How Do
GIANTS FALL?

How Do GIANTS FALL?

EXPLORING THE WORLD OF ANTHROPOMORPHIC EXPRESSIONS

BENJAMIN LEE VINCE

authorHOUSE®

AuthorHouse™
1663 Liberty Drive
Bloomington, IN 47403
www.authorhouse.com
Phone: 1 (800) 839-8640

This book is a work of non-fiction. Unless otherwise noted, the author and the publisher make no explicit guarantees as to the accuracy of the information contained in this book and in some cases, names of people and places have been altered to protect their privacy.

© 2015 Benjamin Lee Vince. All rights reserved.

No part of this book may be reproduced, stored in a retrieval system, or transmitted by any means without the written permission of the author.

Published by AuthorHouse   10/20/2015

ISBN: 978-1-5049-4970-5 (sc)
ISBN: 978-1-5049-4969-9 (e)

Library of Congress Control Number: 2015915095

Print information available on the last page.

Any people depicted in stock imagery provided by Thinkstock are models, and such images are being used for illustrative purposes only. Certain stock imagery © Thinkstock.

This book is printed on acid-free paper.

Because of the dynamic nature of the Internet, any web addresses or links contained in this book may have changed since publication and may no longer be valid. The views expressed in this work are solely those of the author and do not necessarily reflect the views of the publisher, and the publisher hereby disclaims any responsibility for them.

KJV
All scripture quotes within this book are taken from the Orville J. Nave's Study Bible, KJV, copyright, 1907, Moody Press.

CONTENTS

The New Goliath Awaits Book Series vii
Introduction ix
Explanations xi
Preface xiii

Chapter 1	The Language Barrier 1
Chapter 2	Rejecting Knowledge 4
Chapter 3	Exploring The World Of Anthropomorphic Expressions 7
Chapter 4	The Breath Of Life 20
Chapter 5	Where Is God? 26
Chapter 6	Discovering God 31
Chapter 7	God Is A Spirit 39
Chapter 8	What Then Is A Spirit? 44
Chapter 9	No Man Hath Seen God At Any Time 49
Chapter 10	Three That Bear Record 60
Chapter 11	Powerful Nothings 66
Chapter 12	Robotic Bodies 71
Chapter 13	His Body 77
Chapter 14	The Word Was Made Flesh 86
Chapter 15	A Paradox Of Incoherency 94
Chapter 16	Emotional Ecstasy 100
Chapter 17	Utterance Or Mutterance 106
Chapter 18	Decently And In Order 117
Chapter 19	Caught Up Into Paradise 119
Chapter 20	The Witness Of The Spirit 124
Chapter 21	How Do Giants Fall 132
Chapter 22	A Baptism Of Repentance 144

Chapter 23	A Baptism Of Remission – Part One	164
Chapter 24	A Baptism Of Remission – Part Two	175
Chapter 25	A Baptism Of The Spirit	181
Chapter 26	Lend Me Your Life	184
Chapter 27	The Mystery Of The Talking Snake	190

Concluding Thoughts 197
Index 199
Other Books By Benjamin Lee Vince 203

THE NEW GOLIATH AWAITS BOOK SERIES

Ending the year 2001, I felt in my heart that the Lord was calling me into a new era of labor of which I knew nothing about. (This is characteristic of the Lord to call someone into a strange field of labor of which they know nothing about.) Nonetheless, one morning as I awoke to prepare myself for work, the Lord spoke to my heart (through His Spirit) concerning writing a book. While meditating upon this inspiration I said to the Lord, "I know nothing about writing; however, if you will anoint my heart with what you want written, I will do my best to transpose it into a manuscript." Then, instantly, (as we would say in the computer age) the Lord downloaded into my heart what He wanted written. The words, though not yet made known, the essence of the subjects was suddenly revealed to my heart.

Since I knew nothing about computers and less about writing, I needed someone who knew their way through the curvatures of literature, so the Lord sent a prominent orthopedic surgeon into my life to mentor my work. Impatient by nature, and as unapologetic as was his bedside manners, (as he was well known for that) our knowledge factors blended together as a hand with a pen. Thanks Doc for being my mentor; God, you, and me, put it together as a team. (My picture on the front cover of my books was his idea.)

I signed up for a ninety-hour college course in 'Introduction to Computers' and my journey into the world of writing began. When the time came to start the project, amazingly, it was then that the waves of inspirations began to flood my mind. And as the abundance of heavenly thoughts came rushing in, I offered my hands, my mind, and my heart to God for whatever He would run through them to the keyboard.

Over the next three months I wrote from the moment I arrived home from work until late into the night hours, hoping not to lose any of the inspirations the Spirit was speaking. I took notes: I scribbled, I scrabbled, and I asked many questions. Unbeknown to me, within three months I had outlined a series of books, which has developed into *"The New Goliath Awaits Book Series"* surrounding the lives of David and Goliath. Five books are now in print nationally and are available through bookstores/websites/eBook & Kindle Fire.

BOOK FIVE

VISIT: www.goliathbookseries.com

INTRODUCTION

The writings in the book of Genesis are mostly a compilation of many scenarios, which suggest that students who challenge these anthologies are in for a big surprise. It's not only a matter of getting it right, but also of bridging thought-factors so other generations can find their way through the scriptural maze.

If you are not familiar with the word *anthropomorphic* or *anthropomorphic expression*, as teachers of any source: Students, leaders, and especially within the ministry who represent the commendable intelligence of God, you need to familiarize yourself with these words. This is not a new doctrine but an old theory used by the scribes to express the mind of God. The *anthropomorphic* approach to the Holy Scriptures has been around ever since God spake His first words to man. In-fact, almost the entire Bible is written in *anthropomorphic* expressions: *"All these things spake Jesus unto the multitude in parables; and without a parable spake he not unto them"* (Matt 13:34).

Man, from the beginning has used *anthropomorphic expressions* in just about every phase of teaching there is, especially when communicating with the elementary world. All the Old Testament characters ratified their knowledge of God to the next generation through this method. If you are an elementary teacher, a Sunday school teacher, a pastor, a father or a mother, you have utilized its value in presenting your thoughts to the next generation.

In light of your need to familiarize yourself with these words, I am introducing them in the beginning of this book instead of the index. The power you will find behind what these words express will increase your quality of thought and your power of understanding the mysteries behind the expressions. Write their characterization down and keep them handy, as the meaning of each word will suddenly enhance your understanding concerning what God is correlating to man in scripture. Too many Bible students speed-read past so many mystical expressions that are waiting to be discovered, and thus, they take the *Word of God* at face value and never investigate below the surface of the expression.

This book is based on scriptural truths; however, I will be examining theories theologians have disagreed upon ever since there was a theologian. Theories are not scriptural truths; however, as in science, when tried and proven, they do shine light upon subjects of truth. My primary theme is to explore, challenge, and analyze myths and teachings that were and are taught by modern theologians.

As the truth was implanted into my heart by my mentors, so will I write according to their interpretations, along with other fundamental truths that many theologians pass over as pointless. Within my studies, students will find that even the manner in which Goliath fell holds significance to New Testament figures of speech: If he had fallen on his back the student would discover a complete different value within the story of David killing the giant.

EXPLANATIONS

I have placed these explanations beforehand to aid the student(s) in his or her studies.

Encarta World English Dictionary–encarta.com/[1]

ANTHROPOMORPHIC / ANTHROPOMORPHISM:
"The attribution of a human form, human characteristics, or human behavior to nonhuman things such as Deities in mythology, animals, and in children's stories."

THEOPHANY / THEOPHANIC:
"The appearance of a god in a visible form as or pertaining to a human being."

METAMORPHOSIS:
Changing the form, nature, and/or the appearance of a thing or person by natural or supernatural means.

METAPHOR / METAPHORIC / MEDIPHORISM:
1. "The application of a word or phrase relating to somebody or something that is not meant literally but in comparison, for example: *"The serpent said to Eve..."*
2. All languages that involve figures of speech or symbolisms do not literally represent their reality.
3. One thing used or considered to represent another."

ALLEGORY:

"A work in which the characters and events are to be understood as representing other things by symbolically expressing a deeper: Often spiritual, moral, or political meaning…a symbolic representation."

SYMBOLIC / SYMBOLISM:
"Characterized by or involving the use of symbols or symbolism…simplifying a technical expression.'"

PARABLE:
"Moral or religious story(s) used by Jesus in relationship to man and life."

PARAPHRASE:
"To restate something using other words, especially in order to make it simpler or shorter."

PARABOLIC:
"Relating to, resemblance of, or having the form of a Parabola (Where two lines or lives meet and take a turn").

MONOTHEISTIC / MONOTHEISM:
"The belief in One Supreme Deity or God."

POLYTHEISTIC / POLYTHEISM:
"The belief in and worshipping of more than One God."

TRIMORPHIC / TRIMORPHISM / TRINITARIAN / TRINITARIANISM / TRINITY:
"The belief of or in a Trinity (A family of gods–a Triune god)."

(NOTATION LINES ADDED)

_____
_____
_____

PREFACE

In book one: *"Angel-Vision-VS-Television"* we discovered how the theories of *Telegenics* has removed man from a world of reality and placed him into a world of fantasy through the powers of The *TV* or Television. This weapon of mass-distraction has replaced man's thoughts with pictures, which has humbled his mind to idolization–idol worship.

In book two: *"The Bible, Re-Write It Or Re-Read It"* we used the *Genetic Cryptograms* of the body to illustrate how the slightest invasion of changes in the scripture can soon establish a threatening discrepancy within man's thoughts of how he visions God.

We then moved to book three: *"Goliath Awaits–When God Doesn't Make Sense"* and examined the sudden impact trials have upon our lives.

In book four: We examined the subtle power of spiritual and political abuse through the life of a righteous king who turned to politics to hide his indiscretion.

In this book: *"How Do Giants Fall"* we will explore the world of *Anthropomorphic Expressions* and challenge the wisdom and knowledge of students in explaining the mysteries hidden behind the mystical figures of speech.

Though the things herein written are strange and unparallel to the traffic of modern theology, they do offer a deeper understanding of the mysteries behind the expressions. If you are not a deep thinker or studious in the *Holy Scriptures*, this book, for the most part, will challenge your orthodox method of thinking. However, if you will consider the *Holy Scriptures* to be a transcending language handed down from God to man and not from man to God, the mysteries will reveal themselves.

Chapter 1

The Language Barrier

Faith and the language of human beings are incompatible with each other: One is of a spiritual factor for communicating with God, whereas the other is of a human factor for communicating with others of mankind. The language barrier between humans really kicked into high gear at the dispersion from the Tower of Babel. Like so many churches of today that try to build a name for themselves, they eventually are dispersed through the same factor: God has a way of inserting division factors when it comes to proving who is in control.

The language factor is yet today the number one cause of misunderstanding God through whatever method man may attempt to reach for Him. It is a known fact that the gospel is the main factor through which God reaches for man, and likewise man for God (Rom 10:17). God looks at man through His *Written Word*, and man must likewise look at God through the same vision factor. However, when God tries to reach for man, since He is God and is a Spirit, He must redesign His language into simple figures of speech so we simple-minded humans can understand what the Spirit is trying to say. God began transcending His thoughts to man the very day He created him. But man, though he has accomplished much through his studies of God and can now speak many different languages; yet he has not the ability to understand what God is trying to say within *His written Word*. You would think that if God would humble Himself down to speak with man on man's level, that man would aspire to communicate with God on His level.

Since (Gen 1:26) speaks of the image of God: *"Let us make man in our image, after our likeness"* etc. We will challenge this phrase on the grounds that God has no physical image or human qualities. And since *"no man hath seen God at any time"*, (John 1:18) man, through his ignorance, has obtained a rational imagination and assumes God's qualities are the same as his. Remember, it was God who created man and not man who created God. When God created man, He created a new species of creatures completely different from the celestial world of spirits, and man should realize this while reading and studying the *Word of God*. Spirits are celestial (invisible heavenly-dwellers) man, on the other hand, is made on the terrestrial level (visible land-dwellers) and God is trying to bond the two together as one through the power of His *Written Word*; sometimes it works and sometimes it doesn't: We have a God with an *image* but no form, and we have a man with a form but no image.

When God came into this world as a man, it was the beginning of a new prototype constructed of man's material and in man's likeness, but not with man's image. He looked the same on the outside but He was not the same on the inside, and on the inside is where the image of both God and man is found. So, in order for man to be changed on the inside, he must be recreated within–the outside remains the same. The word *image*, in our language, represents our human structure, but not so in God's world. In His world the word *image* relates to inner control and power, and holds no suggestion to physical form as with a head, arms, hands, legs, feet, etc.[1]

Since the Scriptures are continually expressing themselves through figures of speech, parables, and mysteries that relate to the church age, what then is God trying to reveal to us from (Gen 1:26)? *"Let us make man in our image, after our likeness."* Since the word *image* in this setting has no relationship as pertaining to a body, it should rather be understood then, not as a graven image, but as an engraved image.[2] It should therefore read as thus: Let us make man and give him power to rule over all creatures as God would rule. It is not the outer shell that God was relating to but that which is within the shell.

Note also the expression *"our likeness."* The word *"our"* is not predicated where there is but *One God*. Many Bible scholars and students engage into strong debate over this scripture without examination: They try to prove or defend the doctrine of a triune god that exist in three persons: Father, Son, and Holy Spirit. But where there is but *One Deity (One God)* the word *"our"* could only be a figure of speech. I doubt very much that God was counseling with the angels, especially not while Satan was still in fellowship. However, Paul did say that God had a problem of talking to Himself: *"...who worketh all things after the counsel of His own will"* (Eph 1:11). So God could have been talking to Himself. Whatever or whichever, one thing for sure, he was not talking with His Son or with His Father, (Rev 1:6) because the Son did not arrive on the scene until four thousand years later, and if God has a Father, then Jesus Christ has a grandfather and no telling how many other celestial relatives– nonsense. The word *"likeness"* differs from the word *"image"* and is a rendering or expression acquired through his creation: that man should show forth by nature some of the attributes of God. However, until man is born again of the *Water* and of the *Spirit*, the only *image* he will project will be moderately opposite of God's *image* or *likeness*.

Chapter 2

Rejecting Knowledge

In my many years of studies I find dissention and rejection when it comes to revealing new discoveries in the *Word of God*. Not just the *Word of God*, but also within the world of mathematics, science, physics, and even in the world medicine. When something new is introduced to the world, even among high-class intellects, I am appalled at whom and for what reason they so easily reject new findings. Some of the most valuable discoveries, which benefit all of mankind, have taken years before they finally make their way to the surface for public use. Why? Jealousy and not enough prophet or fame has pushed it to the back of the line. However, the real culprit that few will accept for the long delays is ignorance. Yes, ignorance, even among the most brilliant of minds the seed of ignorance blooms and thrives.

To make this short and sweet I will lean to the medical field for an example: I read of a physician: According to the Center for Disease Journal, a doctor by the name of Ignaz Semmelweis, (Ignaz Philipp Semmelweis,[3] (1818-1865) a Hungarian obstetrician…introduced antiseptic prophylaxis into medicine who was rejected for his life-saving discoveries. Something so simple was rejected and held back the process of saving lives. (See index for reference and read the complete story at: wwwnc.cdc.gov/eid/article/7/2/pdfs/ac-0702.pdf).

Can you imagine in the world of brilliant minds that there would be competition when lives are at stake? On the other hand, can you imagine in the world of Divine Theology that there would be competition among the ministry when souls are at stake? Since God is the tree of knowledge, all thoughts and truths proceed from Him. So whether the title is Doctor or Minister, what they learn and know does not belong to them but to God Who gave it. Yes, there have been many mistakes and many false reports, which have damaged the lives of many, some physically and some spiritually. Nevertheless, the bottom line in most all scenarios will likely bear the signature of ignorance.

Somehow I see a silhouette of spiritual ignorance within this scenario of those today that minister the gospel, as they too so easily reject great truths. Theories do challenge the beliefs of many who rest in their knowledge factors. And, yes, today, there are those who refuse to accept new knowledge that is against their old methodologies.

In this book *"How Do Giants Fall"* the reader(s) will find discoveries of like manner that have been set aside by the ministry, mainly for their lack of knowledge and/or their failure to investigate. Appraised theories become proven truths by the evidence of the facts discovered, and it would be to the advantage of Bible students if they would examine them; however, many do not, and their rejection of the facts has resulted in the loss of many souls.

Anthropomorphic expressions are not new doctrinal discoveries but an old approach through which God spoke to man from the beginning. And in the likeness of the doctor's case[3] many ministers, for their lack of understanding in the same similitude of spirit, have rejected great opportunities to learn. Because God's people are known for rejecting knowledge, (Hosea 4:6) I offer a challenge to all theologians to lay aside your methodical and orthodox views and re-examine what is now set before you in this book.

Chapter 3

Exploring The World Of Anthropomorphic Expressions

The study of *anthropomorphic expressions* has been in existence since the beginning of time. Those whom God selected as His holy scribes did their best in revealing the mind of God to man; they wrote according to their experience and knowledge factors of their day, and thus, there were many statements written throughout the *Holy Scriptures* that are hard to understand. However, the meaning can be found behind the structure of the sentence if the student will search deep enough. Most mystified speeches reveal things that have been hidden for ages right in plain sight; though the words look clueless on the surface, beneath are worlds of knowledge waiting to be discovered.

One-thing Bible students must remember and understand as they try to unlock these sacred codes is on this wise: The Bible was written from God down to man and not from man up to God. It was written from God's language factor and transposed into man's language factor on man's level of understanding. After God created man, He also had to create a language, a communication factor for man to communicate with others of his kind. So He created a transcending language to match man's intellect: The language had to be compatible to man's power of understanding of what God was trying to say. God does not speak English, or Spanish, or Italian, or Greek, or even Hebrew. God speaks in a Deity dialect that is unknown to man. This is why the Apostle Paul wrote: *"He that speaketh in an unknown tongue speaketh not unto man but unto God"* (1 Cor 14:2). In reality, man has never spoken to God in His language until the Day of Pentecost. Oh, yes, man speaks to man, and man speaks to God; but it is man's dialect and not God's. The unknown tongues opened up a channel through which man can speak directly to God in His dialect–in His language (1 Cor 14:2). Though God understands all languages of the world, His dialect is still from above and is unknown to man. His language is angelic in nature, and no man has been able to crack the code factors without the Spirit revealing it. (I will be writing about those who have found the secrete codes of the *unknown tongues* further in the book.) When God speaks to man, of whatever nationality or culture he or she may be; He speaks to their heart, because the heart understands God's universals language. The expressions: *God spoke* or *God said*, are human expressions and do not apply or belong to God or to angelic expressions, as their world is completely different from man's world.

Spirits are not human beings and human beings are not spirits. The Apostle Paul made this subject clear to us in (2 Cor 12:4) when he was caught up into the *third heaven* or *paradise* and heard words not lawful to be uttered. This is where the mystery gets sticky and tricky: Since when is it not lawful to speak of things in heaven–or do they speak in heaven, and if not, what then is their mode of communication? It is my belief that what Paul was narrating to us concerning what was unlawful to speak is on this wise: He was not authorized to speak on earth of what he had heard in heaven because he did not understand the strange dialect. The unlawful part belongs to man, and the devil is trying to get a law passed that we speak not in the *Name of Jesus Christ* here on earth, neither by word or deed.

There was a language barrier in Paul's experience that, though he understood several languages, yet he could not interpret or break through the code barrier. It was not what he heard that was confusing, but rather, the style of speech–it was unknown to him. Let's look at it from a human standpoint: When we travel to foreign countries we expect it to be the same there as it is at home, with the exception of the language barrier; but that's not a problem, we find an interpreter–problem solved. But Paul heard a language that could not be interpreted–it was an unknown tongue and its phraseology made no sense.

Spirits are bodiless and do not have the same qualities as humans have (they have no voice box or lungs). Every student of the Bible should realize this as they study the *Word of God*: Spirits do not have equality in speech, not in thought and not in limitations; they live in another world that is unknown to man. Only through our human imagination and what the *Holy Scriptures* reveal can we form an honest opinion. In the spirit world they are not circumscribable; man cannot attach a form to them, and neither can man ascribe to them procreation–they do not reproduce after their kind–this applies also to God. Let me reiterate this point again: God can do whatever He wants to do and He needs no help from our human qualities. Our human features are designed for our procreation, reproduction, replenishing factors here on earth.

So, where then did the 23 male Chromosomes come from for the body of Jesus? This brings up another question: Since neither male nor female contributions were involved in the creation of Adam: from where then did the 46 Chromosomes come from for his body? Answer: Chromosomes are needed for reproduction purposes but not for creation purposes. The laws of creation are different from the laws of reproduction. The creation of Adam was spiritual; however, the creation of his body was physical; when God blended them together as one, the composition was complete: Everything that Adam needed to exist as a human being came with the body. Adam was the seed of man and seeds need no outside properties (Gen 1:11 / 1 Cor 15:46). A complete tree is produced from one seed, after that a forest was born. All cultures were produced from the one seed of Adam (1 Cor 15:38) and by the same token all Christians by Jesus Christ.

When God created the body of Jesus, likewise, He created it with all the same essentials as Adam's body–with one exception: Adam's body was made from the dust of the earth–Jesus' body was "...*made of a woman*" (Gal 4:4). (If the preposition "*of*" a woman had been "*by*" a woman, I could concede that the woman contributed the flesh; however, "*made of a woman*," offers no proof of contribution.)

There was no need of a contribution factor of male or female Chromosomes because everything came within the seed. Just as Adam was the beginning of the creation of the earthly man, even so Jesus was the beginning of the creation of the spiritual man. You ask: What does that mean? It means that God is going to have a creation (in the future ages) that will exist in a spiritual celestial body that can appear, disappear, walk, talk, fly, is touchable, yet untouchable–a body that is limitless like unto His new glorified body.

Angels are neither male nor female: They are spirits created to serve God in whatever capacity He should so choose, nothing more–nothing less. They are spirits sent to minister but not to govern those who are the heirs of salvation–a good lesson for the ministry to learn and to remember: *"For in the resurrection they* (man and woman) *neither marry, nor are given in marriage, but are as the angels of God in heaven"*–genderless (Matt 22:30). You will not find one place where a spirit produced an offspring through the channel of conception–it did not and it does not happen. Procreation was designed for earthlings and earthling only.

Deity is neither male nor female; they do not reproduce, especially not after the manner of sexual intercourse. If there is any reproduction of spirits it will be in the form of an assembly line rather than a nursery. I may expound upon this later if time and space permit. But for now I will briefly go over a strongly debated subject, which is: Since spirits do not reproduce, (I used the word in the singular tense-sense because there is but *One God*). Who then was *The Son of God*?

If spirits do not reproduce, how and by what means then did Mary conceive and bear this Son? Our modern day theologians have conceived in their minds that God had a body up there in heaven. If that were true, why then was there so much interest in the need of Him creating another one for the earth? Reason: God never had a body to dwell in until Mary introduced it to the world. We have allegories, symbols, and hints of all sorts–but no reality to the fact. I could write a book on this one subject alone. However, to shorten this classic paradigm, the answer is very simple yet very obscure, and is hidden from the hearts of those who believe in the theory of a triune god, or a god in three persons. God is not three-in-one or one in three–He is ONE and ONE ALONE. In whatever manifestation He exists or reveals Himself, He remains to be ONE. That Son or that Child which was conceived was not a son of a deity, as in procreation–reproduction, and I can say this without blasphemy against God, the Holy Scriptures, or the Holy Ghost. Oh, yes, Jesus was a Son, and He was called the *Son of God* just as the scriptures says He was: However, the *Son of God* was His codename to conceal His secret mission and His identity from the devil.

This is where we humans go astray with the language barrier: We cannot differentiate between spirits and human factors and their abilities. We think within human terminologies concerning procreation; humans reproduce–spirits do not reproduce. *"For God so loved the world that he gave his only begotten son,* (John 3:16). This is an *anthropomorphic expression* designed to reveal that Divinity and humanity is going to bond together as one and appear on earth. We humans know and understand, to some extent, the channel through which conception and childbirth is achieved, because it happens all day every day with man and woman–but not in the spirit world.

People believe and ministers preach that Jesus Christ was a reproduction of God–this is a misconception within the human mind. God had to make His approach to man through man's fashion so He could speak to man on man's level: *"That which is conceived in her"* is transitive in its nature, (Matt 1:20) and is designed to correlate a message that Deity is coming to town in the likeness of man. But how, through, and by what means is this going to happen since spirits do not reproduce?

This is a mystery that has been a conflict between theologians since it was first prophesied. We could brush this mystery aside by just saying God can do whatever, wherever, whenever, and however He chooses. And, on the bases of how it is written, most Bible scholars accept it that way, mark it as an unsolved mystery, and leave it alone. I cannot rest when a door of opportunity is open and knowledge is oozing out.

All the spirits in heaven and wherever there may be elsewhere, God only knows, not one of them was conceived through a birthing process. Oh, yes, they were conceived, no doubt, but only in the mind of God. Since heaven is a place of invisibleness, there was really no need to create for them a body; that would cause havoc like on earth. The earth and human beings was a new order of creation for God, along with all the other creatures that help groom and maintain the functions of the earth–land, sea, and sky. All creatures/beings both in heaven and on earth were created to serve and to worship the Creator in some fashion. (Yes, even the animals and little creatures that annoy us; they too are busy fulfilling their designed purpose.) If then *"...that which is conceived in her"* was an *anthropomorphic expression,* and spirits do not reproduce, who then was this *Son,* and how was this conception brought about?

This next part the devil does not want the world to know: God hid this secret from the devil before the foundation of the world and he never knew who the *Son* was until after the resurrection; then, on the Day of Pentecost, it was revealed to the world (Acts 2:36). *"Which none of the princes (leaders) of this world knew: for had they (Satan included) known, (who He was) they would not have crucified the Lord of glory"* (1 Cor 2:8). The mystery is not in *God* being the *Son*, but the *Son* being *God* (2 Cor 5:19-21). If, then, God cannot reproduce, who then is the *Son* that was born of a virgin? The *Son* then must have been *God*; who else could have conceived such a candid entrance into this world but He–mystery solved.

The conception was done through Spirit insemination: It was the beginning of a new creation and Jesus was the first of its kind–He was *"the beginning of the creation of God"* (Rev 3:14). People do not believe this reality: If God can create a world from nothing and a man from its dust, then He can create a sperm cell and plant it into the womb of a virgin and introduce himself to mankind as a human being; simple equation, simple factor, simple fact: God Himself was masquerading as the *Son of God* and He pulled it off without a glitch.

All Scripture, from the original Hebrew, to the Greek, to the Latin, and to the English translation, all were written in *anthropomorphic expressions* as an approach to man on man's level. Which means: The *Holy Scriptures* were written with the concept that God was likened unto a human being: in shape, in form, in fashion, and in size. But since God's language is of a Divine nature, it is far above the human intellect and comprehension. Therefore, when God speaks, His language and thoughts must first be transcended down to man's level of understanding; otherwise His story would never be told.

God's language is from above where there are no problems or misunderstandings; however, man's language is from below where confusion of communication exists. And it is the condescending of the language factor from up there to down here that is so hard for man to comprehend. It's not that God has a problem explaining Himself; but rather, we humans have a rough time understanding His figures of speech–are you with me? Understanding God's approach has its reservations when it comes to man's ability to understand His hypothesis of balancing a mutual relationship between the two. God listens to the heart from which the mouth speaketh. And since God is the originator of all languages, the misunderstanding factor rests entirely upon man.

Now, then, there is this question that keeps popping up from the orthodox section that do not want to change their pattern of thinking, regardless of how the scriptures present God. The fact remains that God is not subject to man's elements, shapes, forms, fashions, mathematical equations, nor similarities. God has no body: He does not breathe, neither is He subject to oxygen. He has no hands, no feet, no head, no eyes, no ears, no mouth, no nose, neither is He male nor female–*God is a Spirit* and spirits are genderless–sync this with your mind. God doesn't even have a brain–imagine that: We have a God that created all things and knows all things yet He has no brain. He doesn't need a brain. Brains are for thinking and figuring things out, and since God already knows everything, He has no need to think because He is a thought. (Keep this in mind: From the word, Logos, we get our word, logic or thought–thus, the Logos was and/or is a thought.)[1&2]

God does not experience emotions or confusion, neither does He suffer from exhaustion; he never tires or needs to rest, and He never dreams. Joseph's dreams were not his own; it was God dreaming about what He had planned for Joseph's future. If you are having dreams of doing something for God, it could be that God is planning your future by letting you see it in dream-view. And should your life suddenly fall apart, it could be that God is putting the squeeze on you to draw out of you the talent He has placed within you.

Since all we know about God is from our human standpoint, thus, we assume that God is subject to the same experiences as man. But man must remember: *"no man hath seen God at any time."* The reason the scriptures attach man's qualities to God: Such as eyes, feet, hands, breath, etc., is to lure man closer to Him. Therefore, what is written about God is written in *anthropomorphic* format, on man's level of thinking and not on God's level of thinking. *"God is a Spirit!"* Keep this in mind: *"God is a Spirit"* and spirits have no intrinsic values as pertaining to the flesh. All the above qualities belong to man and not to God. They are correlative expressions that are designed to balance the power of understanding between Deity and humanity; God is speaking to us on our level in relationship to our intrinsic worth and not His.

All the expressions in (John chapter 17) of the Father loving the Son and vise-versa: All scriptures, however, whichever or wherever written, are correlative to our level of thinking and not that of God's. We have no other language through which we can express or ascribe to the Essence of God or His existence other than our own. Therefore, each expression concerning God must be visualized as an abstract statement of concept of what the writers thought God was like and/or what He was saying. This is where the power of *anthropomorphic expressions* is a useful tool in removing the language barriers and/or the figures of speech that keep man and God apart.

When Jesus said, *"My Father is greater than I."* It wasn't that He was speaking of another Deity; but rather, allowing Himself to be a stepping-stone of trust for the Jews to believe in Him as the *Messiah*. He tried expressing Himself to them in a familiar fashion: He tried to get closer to them through the body of flesh like unto theirs–but it did not work. As I said above: All we know about God is what we know about ourselves; the *man* Christ Jesus came to bridge our misunderstanding factors between spirit and flesh.

The above mentioned are all fundamentals to help us understand the difference between spirits and flesh. Thus, all these scriptures that speak in relationship to man are correlative in nature to aid in bringing God down to where man can understand Him. They are factors of transcending speeches from God's understanding down to man's understanding. Man picked up the writings of Moses and began reading into them that God has all the same qualities as himself, and thus, his concept of God being like man has existed ever since; but the fact still remains, *"God is a Spirit!"*

Read what God said about himself: *"For as the heavens are higher than the earth, so are my ways higher than your ways, and my thoughts than your thoughts"* (Isaiah 55:8-9). Notice the great gulf between the two factors: All of God's thoughts and actions: His ways of doing and thinking and speaking and creating, all are above man's intellectual abilities. So, for God to communicate with His creation, the heavenly scribes had to modernize God's form of speech and bring it down to man's level of thinking.

How do you instruct an earthly creature when you are a heavenly Spirit? How do you reach man's understanding when he is flesh and you are Spirit? The two do not think alike, act alike, look alike, and are not equal from whatever angle you vision them. All spirits are of the same in essence. God created all spirits, including man's spirit, from His own Essence: *"In him was life; and the life was the light of men"…That was the true Light, which lighteth every man that cometh into the world* (John 1:4-9). It is the substance of man, (the flesh) which separates the two. "While the aspect of a form of God is called Divine Image, the aspect of function or ability is called Divine Character."[2] But neither will unify until the *Spirit* and the *Word* agree together within man's heart.

The spirit world is completely different from that of man's world. Man thinks and understands within human levels, and also writes within the same collection of thoughts. But when you are a Divine Spirit and you are trying to explain something to man; how do you write it down so he or she can understand what you are saying? Answer: The *Holy Scriptures* had to be written in our earthly language instead of God's heavenly language so man could understand the Divine difference.

This is where and when the *anthropomorphic* system needs to be applied to help the student or minister understand the heavenly terminology. We humans have a communication problem when it comes to understanding God's *Word*. Man has problems enough communicating with man, much less with a Divine Spirit. We did not write a book about God, He wrote a book about man, and placed Himself into that book as the more important factor. Though His book has a divine anointing resting upon it, few readers have a divine anointing resting upon them to interpret it.

God is trying to reach for man from the pages of *His book*, the *Bible*, which is now the medium factor through which man can reach God's Divine residence. God's language was translated by the best scribes of their day. Moses, the scribes, and King James did their best in translating the heavenly phraseologies into our earthly terminologies so man could understand God's theologies. This was all done when the *Holy Ghost* moved upon them. Though they wrote down what the *Holy Spirit* impressed upon their hearts, they still wrote according to their human experiences and perceptions. This is one reason why the new translations of the Bible have not the same inspiration as the King James Version–the anointing is none-transferable.

When the Bible speaks of the nuts and bolts of God in relating to the nuts and bolts of man, it uses *Anthropomorphic expressions* of speech and not a fact of actuality, i.e. Because the Bible says: "*… the year that king Uzziah died I saw also the Lord sitting upon a throne, high and lifted up*" (Isaiah 6:1). Are we to believe that Isaiah saw God who was once standing but is now sitting? 1. Spirits do not stand or sit. 2. My question is this: How can you see a Spirit that reaches from infinity to infinity and beyond? And 3. How can you tell if a spirit is sitting or standing when its borders cannot be measured or seen? This is an *anthropomorphic expression* of transcending mysteries designed to match man's power of comprehension and understanding. The simple fact is: Isaiah had no concept of a Spirit sitting or standing. He knew only what a king looked like sitting high upon a throne, and when he saw this vision of God being lifted up–what we read was his concept of his vision.

All scriptures are expressions of the mind of God reaching for the mind of man, in relation to man and not in relation to God, and likewise wrote the scribes. God narrates within the boundaries of man's elements and nuts and bolts that man is familiar with: In order to correlate the heavenly with the earthly, God does it by rationalizing heaven and Himself as having the same mechanics. He needs no mouth to speak, no feet to walk, no eyes to see, no hands to touch, no oxygen to breathe, and He needs no heart to feel our infirmities; these are all man's elements, commodities, and attributes. The only basics God needs are man's hands: man's feet, man's eyes, man's heart, and man's breath–breathing out the glorious gospel of salvation to a lost world–without which He is helpless.

But man will never develop man into the Image of God until the *Spirit* and the *Word* agree together within his heart.

What then is God's image and how do we acquire it? The *Word of God* is the artist and sculptor of His Image. The gospel transforms man into the image and likeness of God through teaching and preaching; it is the developing factor, which creates Divine qualities within man's heart, his spirit, his nature and his character.

God has put all the visions, mysteries, miracles, signs, and wonders of this age; all has been placed into man's trust. His most treasured secrets have been entrusted into man's care and into man's hands, and it is now up to man's feet, man's eyes, man's heart, and man's voice to express God's concept of love to a hurting world (1 Thess 2:4). God is counting on man (you and I) to be His communication factor to the world. He is counting on His people to figure out the pros and cons of the language barriers that separate the saved from the lost. He has left it up to man to translate it on all levels of comprehension so others will hear and know God on the same level. This is what *anthropomorphic expressions* are all about: Finding the right expression to unlock the language barrier that stands between God and man and others. Are you preparing yourself for the divine task of presenting God in their language?

Chapter 4

The Breath Of Life

The word *breathe* or *breathed* from the Hebrew text is a transitive verb, which means i.e. It is used to instill a particular quality into a group of people, employees, someone or some thing. A transitive verb needs a direct object to complete its objective: When a transitive verb appears in a sentence, especially within scripture, it is pointing to the objective or dominant verb, which possesses the key to the mystery.

In (St. John 20:22) Jesus spoke these words to His disciples: *"And when he had said this, he breathed on them and saith unto them, receive ye the Holy Ghost."* The transitive verb in this scripture is *breathed* and the dominant verb is *receive*. One thing we know, the disciples did not receive the *Holy Ghost* at that time because the *Holy Ghost* was not yet given (John 7:39). Reason: Jesus had not yet been glorified (crucified). So, what is the writer trying to tell us?

Not many Bible students will accept the thought that Adam was alive when God breathed into his nostrils the breath of life; this is mostly because of their traditional teaching and/or their lack of knowing how to rightly divide the *Word of truth*. (The structure of a sentence is very important: verbs are as grave markers; they help preserve the identity of what is entombed. They are as asterisks` within a sentence designed to attract the reader's attention.) The scriptures say it so pronounced that we zip right passed mysteries that are in full view. Adam was very much alive prior to this experience. The mystery we so easily overlook is that he was not a *living soul*; it took the breath of life to make him aware of God's presence; after which, he became a living soul–alive to God. So, if spirits do not breath, what then is the answer to these two instances? One: A transitive verb cannot be used when someone is dead or unresponsive; thus, a transitive verb can only be applied to invigorate beyond the average pace–if you are dead then you are not responsive and cannot be invigorated.

I see this within churches today whose members need their mouths clamped off so God can breath a new breath of life into them through their nose–I think you know what I mean.

You know how the boss does it when production is low: Suddenly, he comes out of his office and calls a pep-rally to crank everybody up into a higher gear so he can get more production. A transitive verb is also used as an expression of encouragement at graduations, to inspire confidence into the graduates as they take on the world they've been studying about. This is what Adam needed before taking on the responsibilities of his world–it was his revelation of God.

This happened to the disciples as they were waiting in the upper room for the breath of life to make them alive with power to preach the gospel. Jesus had one more thing to say to His disciples before He left, and it was all summarized in this one short sentence: *"He breathed on them and said, receive ye the Holy Ghost."* Many of the scribes abbreviated their thoughts as they wrote. It is my opinion that Jesus said more than what is recorded and the above is only an abbreviation. Nevertheless, they did receive the *Holy Ghost* on the *Day of Pentecost* and then they were now ready to preach the gospel (Acts 1:8). (Adam got connected to heaven's WiFi system, but the disciples got connect to heaven's Bluetooth system–try it, it's great.)

Another word supportive to this thought is the objective word *"became,"* (Gen 2:7) which received its power from the transitive verb, *"breathed."* When something becomes something else, it loses its first identity and ceases to exist in its original essence. Properties that are essential to a substance cannot be changed without causing the original substance to cease to exist:

A butterfly was *made* a caterpillar, but it *became* a butterfly by the fact that it was already alive. This is not proof of evolution but merely a revision in God's wisdom, in showing man that he can become something more than just being a worm of a man (Ps 22:6). Adam was *made* a man but he needed his spirit stimulated; thus, he *became* regenerated by virtue of God breathing into him a new significance. *"The Word was made flesh and dwelt among us,"* but it *became* a sacrifice for our sins. The *Word* did not become flesh–it was made flesh. Adam did not lose any of his qualities as a man when God breathed into his nostrils the breath of life; but rather, he became rejuvenated by this life-changing experience–how about you?

Lydia was just a servant when her heart was opened by the power of the gospel that Paul preached, and then she entered into a new dimension of spiritual thoughts she had never experienced before. When Paul spoke to her concerning the gospel of Jesus Christ, her heart was opened and she moved spiritually into a new dimension of responsiveness. After the Spirit breathed into her through the power of the gospel, her life was changed and she *became* a living soul–alive to the *Word of God*. One thing the reader must realize is this: This story is not about Adam and Eve. The writer is painting a picture-story, a blueprint of the creation of the church some four thousand years in the future. As Paul said: *"Which things are an allegory"* (Gal 4:24).

Our old quality of life was not responsive to spiritual things, then God *breathed* the breath of life into our hearts by the power of the gospel and we *became* living souls–alive to God. We did not lose our old flesh, but rather, the spirit within us was awakened to God's Spirit. On the spiritual side: When a sinner hears the gospel, it is God trying to breathe into him the breath of life. *"And the Lord God formed man of the dust of* *the ground and breathed into his nostrils the breath of life, and <u>man became</u> a living soul"* (Gen 2:7). And from that point onward, God did not breathe again until some four thousand years later when He breathed the breath of life into His disciples on the *Day of Pentecost,* and man again became a living soul.

When God breathed into man the breath of life the mystery of salvation began to unfold: <u>*Spirits do not breathe*</u>; they are not subject to or dependent upon oxygen. They are not limited to man's dependencies, such as food, clothing, or exhaustion. I would tremble to think that my God was running out of breath, especially when I was in an emergency situation and needed Him. One thing the student must keep in mind is: The writer of Genesis was painting a word-picture of the church age some four thousand years in the future; all Old Testament arrows point toward this dispensation of grace. Though contrary to many Bible scholars, this author believes the scribes used these *anthropomorphic expressions* to correlate God's thoughts toward the church age. And thus, I am compelled to believe that Adam was already alive and well, walking and talking and eating and breathing when God came to him that day. Another reason I believe this, is because *"...the life of all flesh is the blood..."* (Lev 17:14). Remember: the life of the body is in the blood, not the spirit. When God created Adam's body all the necessary entities' came with the body; including his spirit, which gave his body power to move and to navigate with wisdom and knowledge and vision–all pertaining to this life on earth. But it was another Spirit from above that Adam needed, which he received when God breathed into him the breath of life.

This is not a story of Adam and Eve's natural creation. This story is a correlated portrait of the creation of the church, which God would breathe eternal life into some four thousand years later (John 20:22). Just as the breath of life came after the body was formed, even so the Spirit came after the church was formed. God breathed into Adam eternal life. What was taken from him when he sinned? Eternal life–immortality; replacing it with death–read your Bible! The church was alive and well, walking and talking and doing things after its fashion. But it needed the breath of life breathed into it to make it responsive to God. When Jesus breathed on His disciples and said, "...*receive ye the Holy Ghost*" (John 20:22) this was a prophetic statement of the coming *Day of Pentecost,* because the *Holy Ghost* was not yet given (John 7:39).

Oh, yes, the scriptures do read that John, the Baptist' was "...*filled with the Holy Ghost, even from his mother's womb*" (Luke 1:15). But John was a prophet, and like all prophets, he received the Spirit of a prophet, as a prophet, under the Old Testament Law of prophetic anointing. On the *Day of Pentecost* God breathed into the church the breath of life and the church became alive and responsive to the presence of God–the scriptures suddenly became alive within their hearts. This is what happened with Adam: Suddenly his heart and mind was opened and he became responsive to God.

When the Apostle Paul wrote to the Ephesians concerning the husband and wife being one, (Eph 5:32) he was speaking concerning Christ and the church being one–the Spirit and flesh synchronizing as one. Every story, every character, every creature, every parable, every phrase, every mystical expression, and every mystery within scripture; in some way they offer a chronicle concerning Christ and the church. And it should be the challenge and desire of every Bible student and pastor to dig out the meanings hidden behind these *anthropomorphic expressions.*

If man can understand the process of ingested food for the natural body, why can he not understand the same for the spiritual body? We dig into the earth and plant seeds, which produce life-giving nutrients for our bodies, which transform us into the image of a man. Likewise, the *Word of God* offers life-giving nutrients, which transforms man into the image of God.

Adam's fall sent man away from God, but He did not give up on man. In His efforts to revive man from his unconscious state of mind, He is again using the breath of life technique; this is why the word nostril has appeared in the writings. The word *"nostrils"* is here used as an expression only concerning regeneration; it is in the rebirth or revive tense-sense and not in the literal *snout* tense. The nose is only mentioned to express a last resort of hope when people do not respond to mouth-to-mouth efforts.

God has tried all through the ages to revive man from his spiritual state of mental paralysis. But now, as a last resort, He has chosen again to demonstrate the nostril method on the church and amazingly it is working, because man is *becoming* aware of God every day all around the world through this method. *The breath of life* is the breath of the gospel that men preach and by which men and women believe and *become* living souls–responsive and alive to God.

What were you doing the day God came to you and offered you the breath of life? I can tell you: You were alive to self but not to God.

Chapter 5

Where Is God?

To continue our studies we have obtained permission to use this article: *"Where is God"* written by Jason Dulle from one of his great works on trying to identify God–This subject is one of infinity and must be approached with an open mind.

"Exploring the nature of Omnipresence" by Jason Dulle www.Jasondulle@yahoo.com (Used by permission).[5]

"Prior to the creation of the material universe: (ex nihilo) there was no space or time. Because there was no time, we conclude that God existed temporally (timelessly). What about the absence of space? Would this not mean God existed *non-spatially* (non-active, or relating to space or to the facility to perceive objects in *space–spatially*) without creation? Yes, it would. How does that conclusion square with the Biblical teaching that God is *Omnipresent*? How can a being that is spaceless in nature be *Omnipresent*? Is the Bible contradicting itself in its description of God's nature? What exactly is the nature of God's *Omnipresence*? Has He always been omnipresent? These questions ought to cause us to think more clearly, about what it means to say God is *"Omnipresent."*

To be all-present requires that there be a *"here"* and a *"there"* to be present at. Without the existence of spatial locations, the notion of *Omnipresence* is meaningless. Seeing that there was no space *"prior"* to creation, it follows that God was not

Omnipresent prior to creation. *Omnipresence*, then, is not an essential attribute of God's nature; spacelessness is essential to God's nature. "God existing alone without creation is spaceless." God became *Omnipresent* concurrent with creation in virtue of the creation of space. *Omnipresence* emerged as a contingent relation between God and the *spatial* universe He created.

What then is the Nature of God's Omnipresence?

While we have determined that God is spaceless without creation and *Omnipresent* subsequent to creation, this does not tell us anything about the nature of His *Omnipresence*. What does it mean to say God is omnipresent? Does it mean He is *spatially* (relating to, occupying, or happening in space) located within and extended throughout the universe such that He is present at every point, or does it mean He is cognizant (apprehensive by the mind—awareness—noticeable) of and causally active at every point in the universe though He is neither *spatially* located in, nor *spatially* extended throughout it? While we have typically conceived of *Omnipresence* in the first sense, I would argue that God's *Omnipresence* is more aptly described by the second.

At a minimum, God's *Omnipresence* means He is not localized anywhere within space, and that He lacks both shape and size. However, if *Omnipresence* refers to God's extension through space, He would have both shape and size, because the universe has both shape and size. God is not extended through space so that He fills it like air fills a container. God is not a physical substance that can fill anything. God's *Omnipresence* in the universe is more comparable to the way in which our minds are "*filled*" with thoughts. Our thoughts are not *spatially* extended throughout our *minds*, and neither is God *spatially* extended throughout the universe.

If God were *spatially* present at every point in the universe, He could not distinguish *"here"* from *"there."* For a being that is spatially present at every point in the universe, everywhere is *"here;"* everything is ever-present before Him. There is no *"there"* for such a being. If God were *spatially* extended through space He must believe that two points separated by millions of light years are both *"here."* That would mean God could not know the Statue of Liberty is separated from the Eiffel Tower by thousands of miles. That is patently absurd, and impugns God's *Omniscience*! There must be a better way of understanding God's *Omnipresence*.

Has God Changed?

Earlier I argued that spacelessness, rather than *Omnipresence*, is essential to God's nature. Those properties that are essential to a substance cannot be changed without causing the substance to cease to exist. Only accidental properties can be changed if the substance is to retain its essence. If spacelessness is essential to God's nature, then how could God become *Omnipresent* at creation without giving up the property of spacelessness and ceasing to be who He was? If God's *Omnipresence* is understood as a *spatial* location extended through space, this is unavoidable, for He would be required to relinquish the property of spacelessness in order to assume the property of *spatiality*, and thus, He would cease to exist as the divine Essence He once was to take on a new essence. If, however, God's *Omnipresence* is understood as God's immediate mental cognizance of and causal activity at every point in the universe, then God's *Omnipresence* would not encroach on His essential spaceless nature. Mental cognizance (perception) and causal activity do not require *spatial* presence.

Additionally, there is nothing intrinsic to the act of creation that would require God to be drawn into space by (*spatialized–activated*). Creation was not a spatial act; therefore, we have no compelling reason to believe God surrendered His divine spacelessness and began to exist spatially subsequent to the act of creation. It stands to reason that God remained spaceless even subsequent to creation. If God remained spaceless, His *Omnipresence* must mean He is simply "cognizant" (conscious) of and causally active at every point of space."

Conclusion

God's *Omnipresence* is an example of analogous (similar) language in which those incomprehensible aspects of God's nature are described in terms finite humans can comprehend. We run into problems, however, when we take this use of language and apply it to God in literal terms. God is not *spatially* extended throughout the finite universe, but is cognizant (*conscious*) of and causally active in each and every part of it as a *non-spatial* being. Because God is *mentally* cognizant of, rather than personally located at every point in the universe, He can be both *"here"* and *"there,"* and know the difference between the two.

Footnotes

1. To speak of that which was prior to creation is a figure of speech, similar to the way scientists speak of temperatures "lower than" absolute zero. It is a mental construction only, having no ontological (philosophical) basis in reality. The beginning of time is a boundary beyond which only our imagination can travel. Trying to find time before the beginning is like trying to cross the boundary of space into spacelessness. There is no space on the other side of space in which to cross over into, and likewise there is no time on the other side of

the beginning to go back to. (William Lane Craig and J.P. Moreland, Philosophical Foundations for a Christian Worldview (Downers Grove, IL: intervarsity Press, 2003), 510.)

2. Space was created by God, but that does not mean it was manufactured as if it were some physical substance. To say God "created" space merely expresses the fact that: 1. Space had a temporal beginning, and that: 2. God is its causal agent. Space is not a physical substance, but a relation that obtains in virtue of the presence of finite and material objects. Just as time keeps every event from happening at once, space keeps everything from being located at the same point. In the utter absence of finite and material objects, space would not obtain. God no more created something called space than we create the relation "next to" when we place two books side-by-side. Apart from the creation of matter, there would be no space (or time for that matter). For it is only the creation of material substance that necessitates there be space in which the matter can exist, and time in which the matter can move. Space and time *"came along for the ride"* in virtue of the creation of matter, but they were not the objects of creation itself. The relations of space and time emerged with the existence of matter. Space is a contingent relation emerging concomitantly (accompanying/ attending) with the presence of material substance." (William Lane Craig and J.P. Moreland, Philosophical Foundations for a Christian Worldview (Downers Grove, IL: intervarsity Press, 2003), 510.)

Chapter 6

Discovering God

Greatness found in men of discoveries has not been in their discovery itself, but rather, within their determination and pursuits into the mysteries of unspecified knowledge. It sets their desire afire to reach farther and deeper and higher into nature, culture, science, medicine, and even concerning the existence of God. When someone discovers God it is like entering into a new world of knowledge never realized by its day or time. Thus it was with my life before I encountered the knowledge of the Lord Jesus Christ. I grew up facing a life of poverty and a zigzagging future, compounded by not knowing God or the beauty found in His wonderful *Word*–until Christmas 1959.

I was a young man that was maturing without directions; I needed someone to guide and mentor me in getting an education and securing a trade with continuous employment. My future was without direction, empty and meaningless, and being a young man, I was facing a puzzling future. I remember falling to my knees in private prayer one evening and asking God if He would help me to find Him; if He would come into my life and be my guide, my mentor, and my friend. I asked Him to deliver me from a destination of darkness and give me a life with spiritual meaning–I will not forget that prayer.

I was young and wild, and like most teenagers, I knew everything there was to know. I had a job working at a gas station and I didn't make much money. My car was old and

I loved to street-race on Woodward Ave on the south end of town, especially late at night while the police were changing shifts and not patrolling. It was late in December 1959 and the weather was still good to us lovers of outdoors; a little cool but a jacket, our adrenalin factor, and the sound of squalling tires warmed our blood. God, in His own way had put wheels on my prayer and sent two young men to invite me to their church only blocks from where we were racing.

Don't be surprised if the answer to your prayer comes to you in a strange costume; as God is strange and so are His ways. My fifty-dollars a week job was all I needed while living with my Mother and older brother. My Dad and Mother divorced when I was five and he lived in Kentucky, so I was left alone to do my own thing while growing up–not a good thing for any teenager. Yet, if you will study the scriptures, you will find that most whom God used were just as I.

As I remember: It was late in December and I was street racing these two guys who, as I noticed, were of a clean character and conversation. There are some limits to the rules of holiness, and it would be to the advantage of the more holy if they would get out of their tent and into the main stream of life where sinners roam. After all, many of them, just as I, are looking for eternal life wherever they can find it, and it could be you who leads them to Christ.

After a few runs up and down the strip we stopped to talk about our cars and the pretty girls, and that was when they invited me to visit their church on the following Sunday night–only a few blocks away. I didn't know salvation was so close. They were having a two-week revival the week before and the week after Christmas. Oh, yes, we were breaking the law. But it's sort of like going over into the camp of the enemy and winning one of their servants without getting caught. Plus, we had friends within the department, and if we got caught, we just kept our mouths shut, paid the five-dollar fine, and we were free to go. That's the way it is in the secular world; we can buy our way out–but not with God.

At that time I was attending a protestant church similar to the Baptist church that was not into worshipping God as Pentecostals do. My heart and soul was hungry for the breath of life and I was not getting it where I attended. I accepted their invitation and came to the Sunday evening service, and when I walked into their church I was surprised at what I found. When I walked through the front door the hostess quickly greeted me and said, as if I were their friend, "Praise the Lord, we're so glad to have you with us tonight, just make yourself at home and be a part of us." These folks were warm and friendly, and I must say, they were wild and different in their way of worshipping God. In addition, amidst being a stranger to their ways, somehow I knew I was home; that I had found the church that preached the truth. I felt in my heart that I had found the *"pearl of great price"*–the prodigal had come home. I continued attending the Apostolic Church from late December 1959 until late June 1960 and then my life really changed.

I had sold my old jalopy to my brother, who will never forgive me for rolling up his pant legs to the knees and pawning it off on him. Nevertheless, he recovered from the shiest and let me live–so I was without a car for a while. The girls sure were pretty there at that holiness church, with their beautiful dresses, their long hair, and their clean looking faces that were not all highlighted with betrayal. No need for me to ask them out–I was wheel-less, and besides, the pastor frowned on his girls dating sinners. Nevertheless, there was this one girl (I believe she was God sent) that had compassion on me and asked her folks if they would take me home with them to visit for a short while after church and then her Dad would drive me home. This continued for a few weeks.

Then, one Sunday night after church while visiting with them, their daughter and I went strolling around the block to talk, and did I ever get the surprise of my life. We were just slowly walking and talking about nothing important, when suddenly she stepped over in front of me and asked this question: "What do you believe it takes to be saved?" It stunned me–I didn't know what to say. At that moment I was more interested in romance than I was salvation. After all, I was a teenager with a lonely heart and she was a beautiful girl, and who wants to talk about being born again when there could be romance? Nevertheless, she was more interested in my salvation than she was in my romancing; I should have appreciated her concern. But I was a teen with the mind of a teen. The girls at this church were taught by a strict pastor not to date or marry sinners, and I was a sinner with the mind of a sinner. On the other hand, I also was a candidate for salvation and this girl, her parents, and the pastor was willing to take a chance on me–with reservation. (I truly was not aware of what was about to happen next in my life.)

I said to her "All I know is just believe on the Lord Jesus Christ and I would be saved." (She wasted no time in getting to the point.) She said to me: *"But Peter said unto them, repent, and be baptized every one of you in the name of Jesus Christ, for the remission of sin, and you shall receive the gift of the Holy Ghost"* (Acts 2:38). When she said that–when she quoted that scripture, it was as though she had put the key of the gospel into my heart and opened the door to a world of knowledge I never new before. It turned on my thought factors. It was as though she breathed into me the breath of life and at that moment my heart came open to the gospel and to God.

Like Adam, I was not conscious of God until she breathed the breath of life into my heart and suddenly I came alive! My heart came open! My soul came alive! I saw the meaning of what she said! My life suddenly came alive with thoughts of God, as though someone had turned on a light within my soul! At that moment my heart found what I had been searching for! My blinded mind and my darkened heart suddenly lit up because of what she said: The eyes of my understanding were suddenly opened and I could now see and hear with my heart things that I had never seen or heard before! Oh, yes! I had heard these words before, but my life was dead to their meaning; even though I had sat there in church listening to the preacher for six-months.

After she quoted (Acts 2:38) to me and I responded in my Baptist way, I immediately said to her, "Does you pastor know about this baptism in *Jesus Name* and the receiving of *Holy Ghost*?" "Yes!" She replied. I said to her: "Let's you and I call him tonight and talk with him about it." How strange the thoughts of romance suddenly dissipated from my mind and the thoughts of salvation took control my heart. Being a sinner, I could have been hot with passion; however, after my heart came open to the truth, I was now hot to find out more about this Jesus–the God-man.

We hurriedly walked back to her house where I called the pastor and talked with him about this revelation. He asked me to meet with him in the church office the following Tuesday evening at 7:00 PM. He was scheduled to teach a Bible study that evening at 7:30 PM, but he wanted first to explain to me the meaning of what I had discovered before I was baptized. It would be 9:00 PM before we came out of the office; yet everyone was still waiting for this great event. Unbeknown to me, on his way down the isle to the baptistry the bishop leaned over and told someone, "I am going to baptize a preacher tonight in *Jesus Name*."

He was a wise bishop and well known for his wisdom. He also deeply believed that one must first be submerged in repentance before being submerged in water baptism, which was the first question he asked me before I was baptized: "Have you repented of your sins?" Though I didn't understand much about what he said, I had repented at home while in prayer before God. However, had I known the value and power of repentance, I would have spent at least a week or a month repenting and repenting again and again to fully prepare my heart and soul for this sacred event–O the value of repentance. I received the revelation that *Jesus Christ is God* on June 19th 1960, and was baptized in the *Name of the Lord Jesus Christ* on June 21st 1960. I received the baptism of the *Holy Ghost* and spoke in tongues as the Spirit gave the utterance one month later on July 21st 1960; but not without opposition from my family, my friends, and especially from my boss and previous church members.

Before this visit to the Apostolic Church, I had been dating my bosses daughter, and that created a another conflict of interest–now what do I do? My boss was a good man that had been delivered from cigarettes, alcohol, and cursing, and on occasions would take me with him to father-son banquets; he treated me as if I were his son. After all, we worked together, I dated his daughter, he was nice to me, he was my boss, and the word "son-in-law" might have been in his thoughts, etc., etc. O how I wish I had gotten a good measure of knowledge and common sense along with this gift of the *Holy Ghost*; but God never bypasses the learning process. Perhaps I could have been more tactful when I testified to them concerning what I had found at the Apostolic Church–knowledge really does help, you know, even with having the *Holy Spirit*.

Well, you guessed it–my testimony was a disaster. I was rejected, along with what I now believed–no more girl friend and no more boss-friend–they totally disowned me. Nevertheless, I continued to testify to them, but they would not and could not hear what I had to say. This I do not understand: God had delivered this man from alcohol and tobacco and had cleaned up his life. His home projected a perfect Christian atmosphere and I was sure he and his family would embrace this great truth–but they did not. I had discovered a glorious reality that I wanted to share with them. What I had found lit up my life and kindled a fire within my soul that has not to this day gone out; me, a poor sinner, receiving the revelation of the ages, and it illuminated my body, soul, and spirit. The truth will set you free–body, soul, and spirit–and will also separate you from a lot of people, even those whom you love. Even members of my family said, "Poor Ben, he has gone off the deep end." Nonetheless, or whichever, the Lord blessed me with a different job making three times the money and with a different girl friend that believed the same truth.

At this point I want to mention something that has been a mystery to me: Why, after seeking God so desperately. Why do so many people, after they find Him, why do they suddenly stop as though it was a mere accomplishment rather than a discovery? Why do so many people stop searching after they find this wellspring of living-water, and why the charade as if there is no more to discover? Once we find God it is not the ending of a long search, but rather, the beginning of an endless expedition into a spiritual realm that is filled with treasures of knowledge, gifts of the Spirit, illuminations of the soul, revelations to the heart, peace to the mind, and you become a character-witness with facts and experiences that the world of darkness could never offer or produce. Why do so many people stop seeking God and lay aside the supremacy and entitlements of the world to come and settle for passiveness entitlement? I just cannot understand it.

There is more to discovering than just discovering; it is discovering God and all that pertains thereto. Yes, I have made many mistakes since becoming a Christian, and yes, I have sinned along the way; but when I did, I then discovered that God is a forgiving God. And, yes, there have been times that I have doubted His *Holy Word* and said "I cannot make it; I cannot be a Christian and do these things." Then I discovered He was willing to give me more faith–along with instructions. You will not find the grace of God any other way than through failure–well, maybe through chastisement.

Almost all the heroes of faith reached their stardom through strange experiences; some of which were failures to the core. Some denied Him, some forsook Him, some ran away, some doubted, and some even committed gross sins. Yet, it was only through their failures that they were led to an experience in repentance and forgiveness; after which, they returned to finish the race with confidence that God is a God of discovery and rediscovery.

When I was sick–I then discovered His healing power. When in need of secular help–I then discovered He cared. When in need of employment–I then discovered He could make it happen. When the world turned its back on me because of the *Name of Jesus*–I then discovered He became my best friend. Moreover, when I failed Him–I then discovered the depth of His mercy. We rediscover by starting over again and again and again. You'll only discover and rediscover and rediscover God's love and mercy through getting up, and getting back up, and getting back up again. One Christian said, "He was never down; he was either up or getting up." O the wonder in discovering and rediscovering God again and again.

Do not terminate your pursuit of God because of failures or problems you cannot control. Trials are only a way of adjusting how we think and believe. It's God's way of adding to our *faith, virtue, knowledge, temperance, patience, godliness, brotherly kindness; and charity,"* (2 Peter 1:5-8) without which, man will never grow in grace or know the richness of the knowledge of God or himself.

Chapter 7

God Is A Spirit

We cannot fully understand God unless we fully understand what He is. We cannot fully know what He is unless we know Who He is. We cannot fully know Who He is unless we fully experience Him. We cannot fully experience Him unless we fully obey Him. And we cannot fully obey Him without fully obeying His *Written Word*. And this is when we find: *"...that He is, and that He is a rewarder of them that diligently seek Him"* (Heb 11:6). The first reward you will discover after you believe is the knowledge of Him within the pages of the *Written Word*. For within it you will discover what God has to say about Himself, about you, and about others as partners in His vast kingdom. It is easier to understand God if you can understand yourself, because man was made in the image of God and from His own Essence.

Thoughts are unspoken words that run through our mind: They are like electronic impulses that stand ready to activate our motion and emotion factors. One of man's greatest problem is speaking before we think, and thus, our words are made into a substance that is in no wise like what we intended. Thoughts are only valuable and relative in proportion to the wisdom of those who turn them into reality. David wrote: *"How precious are thy thoughts, O God"* (Ps 134:17). Thoughts are bodiless spirits that roam through our mind waiting to be clothed with reality–and likewise with God: To present His thoughts to man, He first had to clothe them in a language befitting to man's comprehension. Which means: God clothed His thoughts in raiments of temporal passions relative to man's understanding–flesh and blood and bone. This also is relative concerning our walk with God, including the way we think, imagine, and/or express God to others. The way we present God to the world will be how the world will picture Him in their thoughts. Christians must learn the art of painting word-pictures, because religious graffiti will turn people off.

God did not need a mouth to speak to man–He is a heart-talker: He speaks to man's heart and chooses things, which touches the center of man's imagination, from which his emotions surface. God deals more in *telepathy* than in speech therapy; He has many ways of communicating with man other than using words: He uses trials and misfortunes, and sometimes-even catastrophes, depending on the severity of the lesson to be learned and the hardness of man's heart.

The reader may be reluctant to embrace this truth concerning the properties of God: of what He is and is not, and what He has and has not. Let me ask the reader to consider your own heart: Though it has no physical entities, yet through its braille-vision it weighs and refines your every motive instinctively superior to your physical entities. It has no mind of its own, yet its power of discernment is unsurpassed by all sophisticated technologies. Likewise, faith has no eyes, yet it can see the invisible as though it were a present reality.

There are multiple and complex expressions in the Bible that lead the reader to think in the natural tense-sense. However, if you look at them as *anthropomorphic expressions* they suddenly appear as a spiritual portrait relative to man's understanding. If you read the story of creation step-by-step it looks very simple. However, when the Bible speaks of God breathing when He does not breath, (Gen 2:7) our minds become confused. If the reader will examine the verb, *breathed,* he will find that it is transitive in its nature, which gives its flash of fame to the dominant verb, *became,* then the mystery of the account will become clear. There are certain words in the Bible that act as keys and/or codes such as verbs, which unlock certain other mysteries.

The *Son of God* was not another member of the Godhead or the family of God, but only God's method of approach to mankind. God clothed a burning brush with fire and spoke to Moses without it being consumed. The bush was not the substance of the fire because it was not consumed; Moses was the substance of the fire, which consumed his life with a passion to deliver the children of Israel. The news of God choosing him after so many years of doing nothing reignited a fire within his soul like the fire of the gospel; God's voice, like the voice of the gospel, renewed his faith and his calling. Being consumed by the fire of the gospel depends on the substance and the attitude of the person near the flame.

Moses hoped that God would one day send him to deliver Israel from their bondage, and within this strange experience he found the substance (faith) he needed. His hopes were again renewed.

What type of substance will it take to reignite the fire of God in your life? In the Old Testament they lived by sight and then by faith, in the New Testament we live by faith and then by sight. Moses had lost his vision of being used, but like Samson and so many others who have experienced shipwreck, after a period of time his ministry was restored.

I have selected to use again a portion from Chapter Six *"Where is God"* written by Jason Dulle to support this chapter:

"At a minimum, God's *Omnipresence* means He is not localized anywhere within space, and that He lacks both shape and size. But if *Omnipresence* refers to God's extension through space, He would have both shape and size, because the universe has both shape and size. God is not extended through space so that He fills it like air fills a container. God is not a physical substance that can fill anything. God's *Omnipresence* in the universe is more comparable to the way in which our *mind* is filled with *thoughts*. Our thoughts are not *spatially* extended throughout our *mind*, and neither is God *spatially* extended throughout the universe."⁽⁵⁾

A. W. Pink explains it another way: "There is a wide difference between *creating* and *making*: To *create* is to call into existence something out of nothing; to *make* is to form or fashion something out of materials already existing."⁽⁴⁾ The *Word* was *made* from a substance already in existence here on earth.

"*Let this mind* (this thought) *be in you, which was also in Christ Jesus* (Phil 2:5). Jesus Christ was God's thoughts of Himself being made into a substance likened unto man's substance through a body of like substance. This is why I believe that a spirit, including God's Spirit, is like a thought that was made into a substance; Jesus Christ was God's thoughts made into a human substance. I am by no means setting into notion that God is just a thought and nothing more–God forbid. However, to affirm and/or to attest what the *Spirit of God* is liken unto, we must choose an absolute or abstract that has no substance but yet exists, and thoughts are the only thing that exists without a substance–until they are *made* into reality: "*The birth of Jesus Christ was on this wise:*" When the word was *made flesh*, it was God's thoughts being *made* into a substance of reality.

This is why the ministry should portray the *Spirit* and the *Word of God* in a manner, that when the preaching is over, people will have a spiritual substance to think upon. Just as cows need cuds to chew on, even so the mind of the people needs something to think upon. Otherwise, they will be as a cow without a cud: Bellowing and moaning and complaining, and will soon become unproductive busybodies.

Good thoughts feed and develop a good mind, without which, the Christian heart will become a playhouse for evil spirits that will lead the heart astray–Have you experienced this? It is not a matter of controlling the thoughts of the people, but rather, a restraining of their wind-swept intellect from being filled with undisciplined concepts, which leads to confusion and sin. Ministers who refuse to restrain these spirits (thoughts) will, just as Moses, inherit fool's gold. Not only so, within churches where the principles of restraint are not taught and/or applied, it is hard to tell who is in charge. Unrestrained church members invent many heresies, which start as old wives fables and soon end as a true doctrine because the ministry refused to correct the error of their ways.

It is a shame that the ministry must set aside their calling of ministering the *Word of God* to wait on tables occupied by inventers of foolishness. Nonetheless, idol inventions and false styles of worship is in the blood of Gentile people, and therefore it is imperative that the people be taught how to worship, when to worship, how to dress, how to act, and how to talk, even if it means suspending the gospel for a period of time–but back to our thought.

(St. John 1:14) is an *Anthropomorphic expression* written in a language on man's level of thought, and is designed to help man understand the divine medium between God and man. If God had suddenly popped into our world what would we have thought of His introduction? The *Word made flesh* was in no wise a reproduction of God; (as spirits do not reproduce) but rather, "*...the beginning of the creation of God*" (Rev 3:14). What does this mean? Before this time God was literally nothing; that is, He had no substance to present Himself to man. He did not enjoy using fire, clouds, smoke, thunder, lightning, or the prophets to present Himself to man. However, by clothing Himself in flesh and blood and bone, He could now present Himself to man as man; thus His joy was full.

Chapter 8

What Then Is A Spirit?

God is a Spirit–what then is a spirit? Where do spirits come from, how did they come into existence, how do they enter into a body, how do they continue to exist, and do they ever die? Do they not have a human structure as man with arms, legs, hands, feet, eyes, nose, ears, hair, etc., and are they not subject to oxygen and food and the same discharges as man–do spirits experience feelings as man? There is no need of feelings in their world; everything is governed differently. Emotional attributes belong to man because man depends on these essentials to survive; spirits are celestial beings that exist as a thought–they come and go as the wind (John 3:8).

Spirits do not have weak and vulnerable attributes as man because they are bodiless and cognizant; they make their presence known by way of thoughts.[5] And since the *Spirit of God* is cognizant, (as a thought) His thoughts are everywhere. (Being cognizant is to be bodily absent but mindfully present.)

This is how God makes His presence known to the world through Omniscience; His thoughts are everywhere. To find God is to connect to His thoughts, which already exists within the mind of man from creation. God has no need of an audible voice because He speaks to the heart of man where man listens most; He speaks through His Essence because man's spirit is made of the same Essence. We perceive God in our mind, but we conceive Him into our hearts. He is there in your mind right now; why not open the door of your heart and let Him in today?

The expression of voice is used within scripture because we know and understand the sound of a voice. God's voice in relation to ours is heard within our hearts; He has a direct bond with the heart of every man. There are only a few instances throughout scriptural chronicles where God spake audibly. We use the expression that we heard the voice of God. We did not hear the voice of God; we heard Him speak within our heart. This also applies to angels of both good and evil who are also thoughts, which also influence the heart and mind of man.

I have never heard or known of a man saying he heard the voice of Satan speaking audibly. Yet the devil is continually conversing with the heart and mind of Christians and sinners alike all over the world every day, yet man never ascribes human qualities to him–why then do they so with God? Oh, yes, man visualizes the devil in red tights with horns on his head and a pitchfork in his hand. That concept hatched from distorted minds of ancient artistry. We cannot ascribe human qualities to spirits–God's Spirit, angels, or the devil's. Whatever is expressed concerning our qualities offers no proof that spirits have the same. Spirits are not subject to bodily necessities; they are not limited as creatures of flesh and bone. Humans are the creatures in need of a mouth and legs and hands and arms and eyes and feet to move and manage their lives; but spirits need none of these attributes.

You may question these thoughts because of all the statements concerning God having human attributes. But consider this: Though man has ears, eyes, nose, mouth, hands, and feet, etc., he only uses these commodities to function with others of his kind. However, when it comes to communicating with God, man, somehow, bypasses his fleshly entities and turns to his thoughts. Why? Because man knows by nature where God dwells; thus, man knows by nature where to find Him. So, in reality, this proves that man has the same

Essence as God–but by measure. Man's body serves only as a conductive factor from flesh to flesh. Man's heart, however, was created more as a communication center, and if man would only use it as thus, his physical attributes would be more conventional.

Man's body serves only as an antenna and transmitter of his real being; his body is his negotiating factor, which interprets what his spirit feels. It is all accomplished through the body where man's spirit lives rather than on the outside where all his charms are attached. A smile touches the character of another and receives one in return. The spirit of man cannot be seen, yet we see his spirit through his character. We humans can get so caught up in the flesh with our thoughts that we literally forget that we are yet in the flesh. Yet, if we drift away in our thoughts to communicate with God while in prayer, why not accept Him as a thought?

This is one of the most misunderstood concepts of God and the ignorance factor rest totally upon the shoulders of the ministry. They strive to give God a body and place Him in sequence with man's properties, attributes, and limitations. However, God's Spirit and all the heavenly angelic hosts are bodiless, formless, shapeless, breathless, arm-less, leg-less, head-less, earless, eyeless, skin-less, mouth-less and tooth-less, because they exist as thoughts.

The only time they need a body is when they come to visit our world, and it is at that time that they create a *Theophanic metamorphosis* approach, i.e. a body of some type that is used by the angelic world that looks and functions in the likeness as man's; otherwise, man would never know or see them when they come to visit. (Today's intellects would call it a *Holographic* or *Hologram* display.)

This happened in the days of Abraham, Lot, Jacob, Moses and the prophets, etc. They walked with, talked with, wrestled with, and ate with angelic creatures that appeared through this type of approach. This is the type of body King Nebuchadnezzar saw in the fiery furnace with the three Hebrews, (Daniel 3:25). Neither Daniel, the three Hebrews, nor the king had ever seen the Son of God, so, how could they have known who the Son of God was?

King Nebuchadnezzar was a heathen idol worshiper, and idol worshipers believed that their gods reproduced other gods just as humans reproduce children. Nebuchadnezzar thought the forth image in the fire to be a son of one of Daniel's gods. Besides, the *Son of God* did not come into existence until Bethlehem. The true answer to this vision is on this wise: "...*God hath sent His angel...*" (Daniel 3:28.) The figure Nebuchadnezzar saw in the flames was the same type of figure Abraham and the others saw: A *Theophanic* or *metamorphosis* expression from the angelic world and nothing more.

One thing Bible students must keep in mind is: The entire lineup of scriptures are all enter-twined, enter-woven, enter-connected, enter-laced, and enter-locked together as a body with veins and vessels and arteries, which carries life to all parts of the mystical body of Christ (Isaiah 28:10). They are all part of the spiritual anatomy of God coming to and living within man.

So, then, dear readers and students, to construct a consistent and steadfast picture-pattern, we will ask this question:

What relevance does: (Genesis 1:26, 2:7, 3:8, John 3:8, Acts 2:2-3, 38, & 2 Cor 12:4) what part do they play within the diagram and anatomy of salvation–what do they prove?

We shall seek to unravel this mystery from the Garden of Eden, to Golgotha, to the Day of Pentecost, to Paul being caught up into the third heaven, and bring it all together as one glorious consummation concerning the church and the speaking in or with tongues. After all, the church needs to know why they speak with tongues when they receive the gift of the *Holy Ghost*. The mystery started in the Garden of Eden and it all synchronized on the *Day of Pentecost*.

Chapter 9

No Man Hath Seen God At Any Time

We are hearing expressions today from sinners and church members that they have seen God and Jesus, have talked with them, and have also seen angels–now that is being spiritual. This is a mystery to me how terrestrial eyes (human eyes) can see celestial bodies (invisible beings) that cannot be seen. And for a deeper mystery they proclaim that they have spoken with these heavenly beings as man speaks with man. Some even acclaim to have ascended into heaven itself and returned to earth to tell about it–imagine that, they saw God and did not die (Ex 33:20).

Most of the characters I have read about in scripture that saw or spoke to angelic beings were terrified and fall on their face as dead men because of the awesomeness of their presence. Not only so, but even having a vision, though it was not reality, created a fear of dying. One pastor while fellowshipping with another pastor was telling how that some members in his church told that they had seen and talked with angels. The pastor continued: "And I'm inclined to believe they did because they didn't show up for church for several months."

If you really want to see an image of God, take a look at your character, for there you will see Him in reality mode. Whichever way you want God to appear, He will appear that way, because you are the best character image God has of Himself. And when you gaze into the eyes of your reflection, look closely to see if there is any compassion and love for the lost and for your fellow man. Then look also for traits of humility and lowliness of heart, because your eyes are the only eyes through which God has to view the world. Your hands, your feet, and your face is the only visual expression through which God can minister to a lost and dying world–do you see Him within you? How you appear to the world is how God will appear to the world; you have the power to manifest Him gloriously or otherwise. How does He appear now in your eyes since you've adjusted your vision? Church members and church leaders, as a whole, are the only Bible characters this generation will ever see or become acquainted with; do they see God's character image in you?

The *Written Word* and man are the only personifications of God this world will ever know or see. The *written Word* expresses the invisible side of God; but it is man who expresses the visible side of God: His hands, His feet, His eyes, His face and His love; all these attributes of the invisible God are to be expressed through man's physical character image.

Allow me at this time to insert the words of the Apostle Paul, who was faced with the same situation concerning boasting among members of the Colossian church: *"Let no man beguile you* (humiliate you and lure you away) *of your reward in* (or through) *a voluntary humility* (by their boasting of) *and worshipping of angels, intruding into those things which* (they) *hath not seen, vainly puffed up by* (pride within) *his fleshly mind"*, (Col 2:18).

Perhaps I am optimistic concerning heavenly visitations and visions, or, perhaps it could be that I was taught to trust the *Written Word* more than *ESP*. I have met people who made you feel as if you were in the presence of an angelic being. And, on the other hand, I have also met people who made you feel like you were in the presence of a devil, and sometimes it was hard to discern the difference. A great Bible teacher who was reasonable in his teaching and thinking taught me, that only those who are busy fulfilling the purpose of God will be honored with this type of experience, because angels are messengers who are busy ministering to those who are concerned about the Kingdom of God. Not because they are more holy or worthy, but rather, that God had a certain plan or calling He wanted them to fulfill, and therefore, they were granted this rare privilege. My mentor's belief was on this wise: If you saw an angel you were not aware of his presence until he was gone–as in: *"Be not forgetful to entertain strangers: for thereby some* (not all) *have entertained angels unawares"* (Heb 13:2). Notice he said *"unawares"*–Did I burst your bubble?

They appeared in old times as male beings and not as creatures from another planet, otherwise, they were not distinguishable. St. John was no man's fool; he knew very well what he was writing about when he made this statement: *"No man hath seen God at any time"* (John 1:18). And I will venture to say also that not even the angels in heaven had ever seen God at any time in His Essence, because that is unknown and will remain unknown to the world. Only by the coming of the Son (*The Word made flesh*) was God's Essence revealed.

The Body was not His Essence, but His Essence was in the Body expressing God's Essence; otherwise, why would St. Paul have made this statement *"…seen of angels"* (1 Tim 3:16)? Their visit to the place of His birth was their first peek at the One whom they had been worshipping throughout eternity. If the angels can serve and worship God by faith, why is it that man cannot do the same?

Man cannot look upon God and live to tell about it; you must look at God through the eyes of faith with your heart and not with your eyes. Though we cannot see God in reality, yet we can see him through the eyes of faith. Even though the scriptures, multiple times, speaks of man seeing God and/or angels, yet this does not mean that they expressively saw Him or them as the writer affirms. If angels cannot see God, there is no doubt in my mind that humans are not granted this privilege above the heavenly host. God appeared to man by or through an accommodating essence like unto man and likewise did angels. Heaven is a place of angelic life–everyone and everything there is invisible to the human eye. A man may see an angel, but it will be only by a similar condescension of the likeness of his own image. Only the church, the saints of God will see Him as He is; however, that will not be until after the rapture of the church when God shall show himself in and through the glorified body of Jesus Christ.

Angels have been known to appear as human beings and then disappear back into their sphere or world–if I may so express. Their world is not a world of flesh and bone and blood as we humans think: *God is a Spirit*, a heart-talker and a heart-visionary; if man wants to talk with God he must commune with Him within his thoughts, because sometimes his heart can be deceptive (Jer 17:9).

The quotation from (John 1:18) *"No man hath seen God at any time; the only begotten Son, which is in the bosom* (the thoughts) *of the Father, he hath declared him."* God's thoughts were made manifest to man through the flesh and blood of Jesus Christ when He dwelt on earth. Jesus had a perfect understanding of His Deity within but He spoke and declared Himself as man without. The quotation concerning God speaking to Moses as face-to-face: (Ex 33:11) *God is a Spirit* and spirits do not have faces. So what is the meaning behind these two scriptures (Ex 33:20)?

The only face God has for man to look upon is man's face. There was a death penalty attached to those who saw God (Ex 33:20). If there were a death penalty attached to all these visions people boast about today, they would think more seriously before opening their mouths and exposing their ignorance. In these texts, sight means knowledge, which we have received by revelation of the Spirit through the *Written Word*. When I open the pages of God's *Holy Book* (the *Bible*) and begin to read, I suddenly see God at work in His sovereignty. I see Him in the heavens above and in the earth beneath my feet. I see Him in every phase of creation: In the animals, in the birds of the air, in the creatures of the sea, in the beauty of the mountains and valleys, as all declare the glory of God's temperament–but I have yet to see Him in person. I will see Him face-to-face in that world where all who go there will have a new body likened unto His glorious body of whatever nature it will be: visible, yet invisible, recognizable, yet not recognizable, like man, yet like God–man cannot imagine.

But how can man know or see God in His perfect Essence or abstract? By reading *His Written Word*. God made man a little less or lower than the angels, and this should explain to us why man is not capable of knowing or understanding his own essence, much less the essence of the spirit world. If man could understand the essence factor of the spirit world, he might understand, to some degree, how God and the angels function. But until then, we need only to know that "...*he is, and that He is a rewarder of those that diligently seek Him*" (Heb 11:6). Man's problem is, he does not diligently (intelligently) seek Him. God has placed all the characteristics of Himself within *His Written Word*, and has asked man to view Him there; yet man is persistently exploring other options.

Furthermore, the word *"spirit"* has many meanings: Such as angel, soul, wind, mind, and even anger. So, whatever God said or did within His *Written Word* is designed in fashion to accommodate man because angelic creatures think and understand on a different level. When God came into this world, He spoke to us in a condescending language designed for our level of understanding: He used transcending expressions from His world to ours, as St Paul so expressed in (2 Cor 12:4).

In the redemption plan: The Incarnation (God being made flesh) did not take away His glory or His power as God. The glory and power of His Deity was truly and genuinely a part of His human nature as well as His divine nature and power. It was an infusion of Deity and humanity conceived from the mind of God to the womb of Mary. (*"That which is conceived* (imagined) *in her is of the Holy Ghost"* (Matt 1:20). (Spirits do not reproduce; they are neither male nor female–God is neither male nor female.) The *conceived* part is not a sperm cell conception as pertaining to the flesh, but rather, it was done by and through the power of Spirit insemination: It was God's thoughts being made flesh. God conceived a thought and introduced it to the womb of Mary and that thought was made flesh; made into a substance of flesh and bone and blood within the belly of a woman.

(And may I add also, that God uses the same system today in the new birth of the Spirit: Man is conceived (begotten) by the spoken *Word of truth* (James 1:18) and he becomes a new creature through the *Holy Spirit*. Receiving the revelation that Jesus Christ is God is proof of your conception by the written *Word*, receiving the gift of the Holy Ghost is proof of conception of the *Spirit Word*. (I find no other suggestions within the scriptures or from writers who attest differently.)

God was enthused and infused but man is still confused concerning this mystery. The *Son of God* part is where the mystery really gets tricky: 1. We have a pregnant virgin. 2. We have a child born of a virgin. 3. And we have a Spirit that does not reproduce. Question: Is the child the *Son of God* or the son of man? Answer–Both and Neither. If the *Word* was *God* and the *Word was made flesh*, then the sperm must have been the *Word of God* and the *Son of God* must have been *God*–figure that one out. Though the *Word was made flesh* through the same process of human birth, the child was not an addition to God, but rather, the beginning of a new creation of God–God created Himself and He used man's likeness and style of material as His physical visible substance. Now that is some God, that He would make Himself known to His creation through their own substance and on their level–but man is still blind to this great truth.

There is a difference in being a son and a new creation. And may I add: There are some creations that man has given birth too, not in reality, but in a figure of speech. Jesus Christ came to be known *as* the *Son of God* and He was called thus by reason of His being born of a virgin. However, the *Son* part was His disguise; God was on a secret mission and no one knew but He Himself (1 Cor 2:8). The birth part was not an offspring of God, but rather, the beginning of the creation of God as a new type of being. *God is a Spirit* (John 4:24) and spirits are thoughts that desire to be perceptible and touchable in the physical tense-sense. If it had been an offspring of a Deity then we could truly say that Jesus was the *Son of God*. However, all the expressions of the Father loving the Son and the Son loving the Father in (St. John chapter seventeen) are *anthropomorphic expressions* of God's love to usward (Eph 1:19) as the love of a father to a son and vise-versa. They are correlating statements made to associate a relationship between God and man. The writings are not exclaiming a Spirit to spirit relationship, but rather, a Spirit to flesh and flesh to Spirit relationship on the bases of a father and a son. The Son part was instituted as an example of God's love to man so that man could become the sons of God through the Spirit; it is an elementary expression designed for man because man is by nature elementary.

The Apostle Paul offers to us a clear explanation concerning this mystery: *"To wit,* (to understand) *God was in* (inside) *Christ, reconciling the world unto himself"* (2 Cor 5:19). It cannot get any more down-to-earth than this. God was inside Jesus Christ, not as a being inside a being, but as using His Essence to fill and display His new design of a man as a man. The shell without–His Essence within: Walking, talking, speaking, looking, feeling, healing, suffering, and reconciling the world unto Himself. The Father was the Son and the Son was the Father, reaching for man as man.

Those who pretend to possess the knowledge of the Essence of God should first examine His Deity before trying to subject Him to the powers and processes of human reasoning. *God is a Spirit* and spirits cannot be divided. This is how and why human beings attach a body to the Spirit; they do not know or understanding that God cannot be divided or circumscribed; we dare not make Him more or less than what He is.

While Jesus spake in a lowly and humble fashion as man, He also spoke as the prerogative of God: He spoke in a spirit of condescension to accommodate the lowliness of man, because man is human and his understanding is precarious and vulnerable. Jesus had to speak to man as man and not as God, because man thinks on man's level. It's not that Jesus turned off His Deity when speaking to man and turned it back on again when speaking as God–absurd. God has tried to speak to man throughout the ages of time, but man could not comprehend His character of thought. The *Word* being *made flesh* was God's new method of secretly characterizing Himself for the purpose of redeeming man on man's level.

God is without origin and therefore is nameless; He could not even name Himself; only by the expression *"I am that I am."* As creator of all things He may be best called Father. And as Father, He cannot leave His dwelling place in the heavens above because He is *ubiquitously* (universally present–you cannot go somewhere if you are already there). Agnostics try to limit God's Divine Being by circumscribing His sphere of dwelling and His activities. In their frenzy of puzzlement to separate the finite from the infinite, they have themselves become confused. And in order to conceal their ignorance of God, they create deity fantasies, which has exposed their lack of knowledge. Oh, yes, man has seen angels, and man has seen God, but only through a condescending *metamorphosis* nature designed to accommodate man's nature and design. There is no need to see an angel when we have the *Written Word* to instruct us. There is no need to see God when His *Word* is written within our hearts. However, if it is not written within the heart, man will by nature seek a physical form to worship.

Angels are sent to minister to man in the nature of encouragements, and, perhaps in the form of protection from harm. They have no evangelistic calling nor can they declare anything to us concerning the secrets and mysteries within the redemption plan; their calling is to minister to those whom God has chosen and to help them fulfill their calling. To declare that an angel has revealed spiritual secrets concerning the plan of salvation–angels are totally oblivious of this database. They cannot utter one word concerning it, because they and the devil are in the dark when it comes to revealing the mysteries that have been kept secret *since* the foundation of the world. The mysteries and secrets belong only to God and man is the only creature that is authorized to explain them (1 Cor 4:1).

Not much of an encouragement to know that man is all God has to get the job done. Nevertheless, and regardless of how lowly a state of mind and body man may be, he is still all God has to depend upon when it comes to spreading the glorious gospel of salvation; God is depending totally upon man and man alone. It's not our looks, our wealth, our speech, or our ability that He needs, but our availability. God made Himself available for us; can we not make ourselves available for Him?

When those great Icons of the scriptures spoke of angels standing by them, they saw them through the eyes of faith, just as though they were there in human form–spirits cannot be seen! Those who were granted a classified privilege of seeing God, such as Abraham (Gen 18:2), saw only a condescending nature and not His real Essence, because *"no man can look upon God and live"* (Ex 33:20). A well-known minister once asked a new acquaintance if he believed in heaven. His reply: "Yes, I was just there this morning and plan to visit there again later today–in prayer."

Not too many Bible characters were granted this privilege of seeing, as it were, an angel. However, those who were granted this privilege saw them in their condescending nature or form (as man) and not as spirits. Angels are ministering spirits (thoughts) that are sent to minister (physically and spiritually) to the heirs of salvation in many different ways according to the needs. Although spirits cannot be seen, yet I have seen many spirits being projected by people–some good and some bad; I did not see their spirit itself but only its manifestation.

"No man hath seen God at any time." This means and includes: Adam, Noah, Abraham, Moses, Isaiah, Jeremiah, Ezekiel, Daniel, and even John, the revelator. You cannot see the un-seeable. Oh, yes, preachers preach that Moses saw the hind-part of God; but what did he really see? Readers of the scriptures, including myself, have believed and have read into the scripture that Moses saw a profile of the backside of God–we all have been wrong. The scripture plainly expresses what God let Moses see: *"And he said, I will make all my goodness pass before thee…"* (Ex 33:19). Moses thought he would see some type of human features like unto himself; however, he saw only the goodness of God. So, what is this story relating to us today? That even when God has His back to us His goodness is still visible: *"…and we beheld his glory,* (not as if, but) *as of the only begotten* (visible DNA) *of the Father…"* (John 1:14). The only image of God that man will ever see will be the glorified body of Jesus Christ and He has ascended up into heaven out of sight–boasting is excluded.

On our side of the tracts: Until the rapture of the church takes place, our bodies and our lives are all God has to express His personality and plan of salvation to the world. On the other hand: I do feel that many a Christian has shown the world their backside instead of the face of Jesus–I think you know what I mean.

One final note: We read of the New Jerusalem having walls of *jasper*, gates of *pearl*, and streets of *gold*. Angelic beings have no need of these things; they move as the wind, over, through, and around. So, why the need of walls of Jasper, gates of pearl, or streets of gold–why walk when you can fly over, around, and/or through? No scribe had ever seen a city of this nature. So, within their collection of thoughts and experiences, this was as close as they could get in describing their vision. As for man seeing angels: It is not that angels appear in reality, but rather, God opens man's eyes for the occasion.

Chapter 10

Three That Bear Record

> *"For there are three that bear record in heaven, the Father, the Word, and the Holy Ghost: and these three are one"* (1 John 5:7).

This scripture has been a brainteaser for many a minister in their studies concerning the *Deity of God*. Like so many other scriptures, God's Deity is hidden from the carnal mind with riddles and expressions that hide His identity, and thus, like idol worshipers, the carnal mind believes there is a family of god's. What Bible students need to remember is this: *"Hear, O Israel: the Lord our God* (is) *one Lord"* (Duet 6:4). There never was nor will there ever be more than *One* eternal *God*–all others are temporal. Regardless of how the scripture may paraphrase its speech, the only equation factor within the Godhead still remains *One*.

To the ministers who quote this scripture, let me ask this question: *"And these three are one"*–These three–Who? And *"… these three are one"*– One what? Are we to believe that these *"three"* mentioned herein are three gods, three deities, or three spirits? God forbid. The devil himself would laugh at the idea. These three then are what? One thing for sure, the subject in view is in no wise pointing to the *Father*, the *Son*, or the *Holy Ghost*. This is a great example of wrongfully dividing the word of truth by three factors instead of one factor. But one what? If the student(s) would carefully examine the subject in view he would find that the writer is talking about *records*: Three records–and these three records are one.

True, the recordings that bear record are of God, but in no way do they point to Him through a division factor because Deity cannot be divided. A carnal mind could easily pull from this scripture a trinity, but then God has no knowledge of a trinity. So, then, it is man in his carnal state of mind who has envisioned a trinity. Are we then to believe that these three that bear record in heaven are one Spirit divided into three classifications of Father, Son, and Holy Ghost, or three Spirits making up One Supreme Being? Absurd. This statement calls for a scriptural clarification.

It is strange, but have you noticed that the Son is not mentioned in this group of whoever is bearing record? It seems to me, that if the Son were equal to the Father and to the Holy Ghost, surely He would merit equality in recognition; however, equality of Deity does not exist, not in heaven or on earth. (The words *Deity* and/or *Godhead* are the same in use, in expression, and in definition–they are synonymous.) But this is in no wise the subject in view. There can be no equality concerning the Godhead when there is but One God: One Deity = One Spirit = One God–no predication, no competition, no opposition. No matter how the numerical factor is computed or correlated, One God will always be the final answer. The first commandment is: "*Hear, O Israel: The Lord our God* (is) *one Lord*" (Deut 6:4). This is a simple fraction with one common denominator–<u>GOD</u>. The only denominator, common denominator, division-factor, or what have you, God is it. The only way any Bible scholar, minister, student, or common man can rightly divide the *Word of truth* is by its own common denominator–the value of One = One.

For example: "*Who, being in the form of God, thought it not robbery to be equal with God*" (Phil 2:6). The equation factor is an *anthropomorphic expression*, which leads the carnal mind to believe there is a division within the Godhead. And since most Protestant students believe in a trinity, they automatically divide this statement by three, and thus, they come up with a plural resolution. However, if you divide it by Biblical math, *One*, you will find that equality is not predicated where there is but *One*. And where there is but *One*, (God) there is no competitors to be equal too, because, whether in the Spirit or in the flesh, you are still the only Supreme God.

There is no equality to worry about, to compete with, to be compared too; nor is there reason of treason when equating yourself as God when you are God. It is a simple equation with a simple answer that these three are records of *One God*. The answer to this scenario is found in the second phase of the same verse: *"There are three that bear witness in the earth"* (1 John 5:8). Any Bible student with just a small amount of studies should be able to see that God has manifested Himself many times, yet the equation factor remains the same.

Though the scriptures speak of the Son existing *before the foundation of the world*, yet we have no record of Him being there. We have a testimony but no record. If the Son had been there surely He would have been on the record books. A testimony is not the same as a record: A record is a validation of proof, whereas a testimony is the word of a witness–but we have neither or. Where then are the proofs and the witnesses to dispute the record?

We know beyond doubt that there is but *One God* and *His Name* is *Jesus* the *Christ*. Whether He is on record as the *Father*, the *Word*, the *Son*, the *Holy Ghost*, the *Holy Spirit*, *Jesus*, or *God*; there remains to be but *One* on record, which agree on this one thing, that there is but *One God* Who is bearing record of Himself. Sometimes He is recorded as the *Creator*, sometimes as the *Father*, sometimes as the *Word*, sometimes as the *Holy Ghost*, sometimes as the *Holy Spirit*, sometimes as the *Son*, sometimes as the *Comforter*, and sometimes as the *Judge* of all the earth; yet the record still bears witness to only *One God*.

Whether God is in His office as *Father*, whether He is transcending Himself to dwell in the flesh on the earth as a *Son*, or as the *Holy Spirit* within the hearts of man, it remains to be the record of *One God*. It is not a record of God the Father, God the Son, and God the Holy Spirit, but a record of God (.) period. We have it on record in scripture that *God* is the *Father*, and that *God* is the *Word*, and that *God* is the *Holy Ghost*–it is a record and it is recorded in heaven. It is not the record of three of any type, shape, form, or fashion, but is of *One God* and *His Name* is *Jesus*.

No Oneness minister should ever allow the insinuation to even pass through his lips or across his pulpit that these three are one, as in three-in-one; not even from the choir loft in songs. There was not, is not, has never been, nor ever will be a "three in one" Godhead. God does not know of a "three in one trio" and man, especially Oneness Pentecostal ministers, should never entertain the thought, regardless of how the scripture expresses itself.

Another surety that we have is on this wise: It cannot be a recording of God, the Son, because there is no God, the Son, just as there is no God, the Holy Ghost; as if there were a family of god's.

One great truth the early church reformers overlooked when they broke loose from the Roman Catholic Church is this: Deity cannot be divided into any division factor other than One. The Roman Catholic Church in its infancy: Their leaders who were pagan worshipers, thought in terms of their gods having off-springs and immediately conceived in their carnal mind an entire family of gods. However, they failed to understand that God is not subject to any mathematical equations, not in heaven nor in the earth. Even He Himself, Who has all knowledge of all things, creatures, angels, and spirits, knows of no other God than Himself.

The thought of and/or the expression of the theory that there are three Deity's: God, the Father, distinct, God, the Son, distinct, and God, the Holy Ghost, distinct, is of pagan descent and was introduced by the Roman Catholic Church when in their formation around the year 300 AD, and was established as their doctrine and enforced by their clergy by the year 325 AD. In the year 1517 AD when the Protestant movement liberated itself from the Catholic dogma, without careful examination, they took with them what is known today as the doctrine of the trinity. This is not a hidden piece of information; you can find this truth carefully documented in most all encyclopedias and world history books as they bear it on record.

The best way to think upon this subject is to accept the fact that the *Holy Spirit* is the witness and the *Written Word* is the record. Another way to think upon this subject is on this wise: We have books with titles, we have subtitles (themes), and then we have chapters, (division factors) which act as explanation factors. The title and the author remains the same from beginning to end, but the theme is examined from many different standpoints within the chapters throughout the book.

God has authored a book entitled *"The Holy Bible"* and His theme is about Himself coming to earth to redeem man from his fallen condition. Within His book He plays many different roles, which best suits His fancy and/or complements His secret mission. Sometimes He plays the role as a *Father*, sometimes as a *Son*, and sometimes as a *Divine Spirit*. All the parables are like chapters through which God expresses His secret mission up close, yet never revealing Himself openly. His mission was redemption, His disguise was His flesh, and the devil never discovered His identity until after His mission was finished: *"for had he known who He was he would not have crucified the Lord of glory."* But now that His secret mission is over and the mystery of God has been revealed to the world; the final chapter is not finished as yet. God is patiently waiting to add your name to his great cast of believers; why not let Him write your name in His book of life today?

Chapter 11

Powerful Nothings

Man is not free in his body until he is free in his mind. To understand this mystery we must choose something comprehensible within our range of thoughts if we wish to initiate and complete our pursuit of God's Essence. Though we can only explain God from our human point of view, our thoughts are used to transmit our feelings, without which they would never develop into reality. Though man is alive within his body, without God he is spiritually dead. And as strange as this may sound, God, without man, does not physically exist. A fearful and bold statement to make, but when you think about it, it does hold a great truth. For spirits to be active in this world they must have a substance through which they can function. This is why they are continually trying to find an entrance into our hearts through which they can influence and take control of our lives–good or evil.

Just as *"Faith cometh by hearing"* (Rom 10:17) likewise spirits, evil and good, enter through the same gates; they enter into our lives to set up a kingdom of rule: Whether it is God's Spirit or the devil's spirit, each enters by and through the same principle factors and for the same reason. Whatever man's sense factors come in contact with is turned into thoughts and actions, which control our emotion factors: If we entertain righteous thoughts we will respond with righteous deeds. If we entertain evil thoughts we will likewise respond with evil deeds. This is why there is a continual war going on within our mind; it is a thought war of evil verses good. Evil spirits have been known to invade even the mind of animals and take control of their lives, so they are not particular of who or what they have for supper (Matt 8:31).

Since, then, these spirits have no substance of their own, they must obtain a substance: A physical body to maintain their maneuvers of evil and/or of good. All spirits work through the same stimulus factors; what influences man's spirit is what influences his deeds. And I must say, evil spirits seem to be establishing their strongholds much faster than good, because man is on a downhill run to do evil.

I will now make another bold statement concerning God's Spirit–It is without substance. Moreover, God has never had a substance until He displayed Himself as man. The Spirit is not His substance because spirits have no substance–the Spirit is His Essence. The essence of physics is found within the nature of its substance. Thus, the Essence of God within man is found within the nature of man's character. As perfume exudes the essence of its extracted substance from the flowers, even so the Essenes of God is found within the substance of the gospel, which exudes the Essence of God's character. The spirit of man is the essence of man, just as the Spirit of God is the Essence of God; God's Essence and man's essence are the same; the soul of man is the essence of man. The essence of Adam did not go astray in the garden; it was his heart that turned away from God and his mind followed.

Oh, yes, God appeared at times to certain people, but that was not His Essence or a continuing substance. God's only substance from eternity to eternity was and is found in the *Word made flesh*. Though God fills all things with His Essence, He never had a substance before Bethlehem. This is why I believe that God's Spirit is like thoughts, because thoughts have no substance until they become a reality.
(5) (We cannot declare that spirits are like shadows because they are immaterial, insubstantial, and depend upon light for

their existence.) Shadows are influential, stretchable, sizable, moveable, touchable, frightening, and even have power to heal, (Acts 5:15) yet are without substance; they, like thoughts, need a substance to function through and exist.

There is an old expression from years past: "That thought has substance." However, thoughts have no substance until they are put into action through human resources. This is why God, though as great and powerful and unsearchable as He is, He still needs someone through which He can reach out and touch the world–don't you want to be that someone?

Words are powerful nothings that can have a whirlwind affect on our disposition. Be they sweet or sour, like the sound of music, they can change the octave of our moods and have an influential affect on our lives.

Thoughts are not necessarily words until they are spoken. We think a lot of words without expelling them. We use them as a medium to arrange what we want to say or do. God had thoughts of becoming a man before the foundation of the world, but they did not mature into reality until the day Jesus Christ was born–then His thoughts were made into a substance–flesh.

The scripture concerning the *"word was made flesh"* which John wrote about in (John 1:14) is an *anthropomorphic expression*: It was written in our language and on our level of thinking. We humans have not yet made the transition from flesh to spirit, and we certainly do not live in the heavens at this time (though some people feel they do). *God is a Spirit* and spirits do not reproduce. However, man is productive, and this is why God made His approach in this fashion–in the form of a son. Spirits do not have offspring–human beings have offspring. God had to explain His coming into this world through our fashion of birthing. But how was the *Word made flesh* through birth?

God tried many times to make Himself known through many people and other visible passions: The clouds, fire, water, smoke, the wind, the patriarchs, the prophets, priests, and even kings, etc. But none of these answered His criteria to reach for man. What He really needed was a human body like unto our human bodies, with the same weaknesses, attributes, and frailties. God's answer to this impediment was He Himself coming into our world, through our means, made of our substance, in our likeness; though weak, frail, and sinful as we were–we had what God wanted and needed–isn't that encouraging–God, needing man?

And dear friend, your life also has what God is looking for. He is searching for someone who will lend Him his or her life through which He can make Himself known to a lost world. Your feet and your hands can be God's feet and hands. He is not concerned about your size, color, culture, or nationality–just any *body* will do. This is why I believe that God's Spirit is like a thought, because once you receive the revelation that Jesus Christ is God, your thoughts will become His thoughts, and His thoughts will become your thoughts, and your thoughts will start working in harmony with His thoughts, and His thoughts are always on reaching the lost with the gospel, because the gospel is God's Essence and substance here on the earth.

Why do we go to church? To gather spiritual thoughts that will feed our souls and help us live our lives in a Christ-like manner. When the enemy comes in like a flood, what does he attack–our thoughts. From where do we raise up a standard against evil–our thoughts. From where do we wage war against Satan's attacks? Our mind. What is taken captive at Satan's will? Our thoughts. The soul of man is nourished by thoughts; whether good or evil, thoughts turn us on or turn us off, imprison us or set us free. Man's greatest battles are won or lost within the margins of his mind; his thoughts bring him victory or defeat, frustration or peace. Eternal life comes to us all wrapped up in thoughts as a gift from God through the voice of the ministry. Man's actions and reactions, whether good or evil, are the results of what he is thinking–his thoughts control his life. The war between good and evil is a war for the control of man's thoughts, because man's mind is a direct line to his heart, through which emanates the issues of his life. Therefore, we do not need to rattle heaven's gates by physical adulations to find God or to get His attention; He is as close to us as our thoughts.

We can never with our finite mind come to a conclusion of what God's Spirit or His Essence really is. However, because God spake through the mouth of Hosea the prophet and said: *"My people are destroyed for lack of knowledge,"* (Hosea 4:6) we conclude then that He was talking about His people being empty-headed. Which means: Man grows in grace with God when man increases in knowledge of God.

So what's wrong with believing that *God's Spirit* is likened unto a thought? Many ministers preach that God's Spirit is nothing but a song and a dance, a jerk and a jump and a shout–so why not a thought? *"…bodily exercise profiteth little: but godliness* (knowledge) *is profitable unto all things* (1 Tim 4:8).

Christians should be very carful of what they think and say, because thoughts turn into words, and words, like spirits, have an affect on other people; they have power to give life and they have power to take life–even eternal life.

_____
_____
_____
_____
_____
_____
_____
_____
_____
_____
_____
_____
_____
_____
_____

Chapter 12

Robotic Bodies

A great way to start a Bible study is to read your text and then start talking about *Robotic Bodies*. Though strange and questionable, the subject is very befitting with today's technology–so let's get started.

Seventy years ago man could not imagine that some day a robotic body would replace him on the assembly line and do a better and more efficient job than he–that day has arrived. Technology has brought us to that day and beyond, and these metal creatures are now performing with untiring precision. They work without insurance, coffee break, lunch, or vacation, they never leave their station, (except for repairs) and they work any and all shifts without sleep or complaints.

From where did all these iron creatures evolve? It all began when man discovered how his own body functioned and what motivated it. Though the human body functions in similarity to these tin creatures, the power sources and properties are somewhat different. These tin-men are controlled through electronic impulse. Man, however, is controlled by a different power source and that is his spirit. Medical Science has caused a dead body to move simply by the use of electronic impulses. But that was the end of their research; the body remained dead and motionless. They have never been able to restore man's spirit because it is man's spirit that makes his body respond. Every movement and every twitch of the robot depends on electronic signals. The human body is likewise dependent upon its spirit's impulses as its source of commands, and it all comes through man's thought system–the heart and the mind.

Spirits do not come in sizes; though they are not subject to dimensions they do adjust for the occasion of the thought. On the natural side of mathematics: For the demonic tomb dweller to have 2000 demons within his body (Mark 5:13) each one would have been the size of a French fry (according to the average size of a man's body). But when they were cast out and sent into the herd of swine, (of about 3000) the ratio suddenly changed to accommodate the number and size of the swines. We cannot measure spirits by size unless it is within man's thought factors; this may hold a great truth as some men think big and some men think small. The adjustments were made according to the thought factors of the swines and not by their number or size–they do have a mind and they do think.

The student must keep in mind that *God is a Spirit* and His Spirit is immeasurable, whereas man's spirit is not. However, in the likeness of God's Spirit, man measures other spirits, which struggle within his mind according to the effect it has on his life. Spirits are always in quest of ways to control a body–any body, anywhere, anytime, even swines. God's Spirit is boundless, bodiless, and limitless, whereas man's spirit is limited to his tiny space of being, which God has so designed.

I like to think of it on this wise: For every movement of man's body an impulse receives a command from the heart and/or the mind, but identifies and refines its source through man's knowledge factors: How much man knows is then evaluated through the channel of his experience and is then put into action. The body of the spiritual man responds in like manner: The force and style of a Christian's response to the world around him will be according to his knowledge and experience factors. God created man and placed a portion of His Spirit within him and He expects man to respond in the likeness thereof and not as fools. Man will give an account to

God for the *quality* of what he knows as well as what he knows (Matt 12:36).

There was a large host of good spirits in heaven that revolted against God and lost their fellowship card. They were then cast out of heaven into this world and are today attacking the thoughts of man's heart at random (2 Tim 2:26). Having no substance of their own they seek shelter within the thoughts of man. The reader may consider this thought to be foolishness. Nevertheless, you will notice that the tomb dweller was well balanced until an evil thought took control of his mind. And if you think that an evil thought cannot take control of your mind, you need to take a rest on the couch and let the kind doctor hear your story; it is happening every day to millions. But notice also: As soon as the evil spirits were cast out, the man regained control of his thoughts and his life (Mark 5:15).

Satan is not omnipresent but is limited as in "...*going to and fro in the earth*" (Job 1:7). Whereas God's Spirit is everywhere present and needs not to travel to and fro to find man, because man is always within His thoughts. This also is another reason God has no need of a mouth to speak; His thoughts are everywhere. Mouths are for directing sound waves to a point of interest that relate to creatures with limitations. God has no limitations; therefore, His thought is His voice. I guess we could say He is like surround-sound–He's all around us and we are always on His mind.

A man's world is only as large as his knowledge factors: Though the sphere is the same to all, the explorations differ because knowledge factors differ. You've heard the expression: "They live in a small world." It's their knowledge factor that makes their world large or small. This can also be applied to how big God is to a Christian. Though our knowledge of Him does not increase or decrease His attributes, it certainly does make a difference in the scope of our faith. What we know of God determines the power of our faith in God, which increases and/or decreases according to our knowledge of Him. Faith is measured by the nature of a grain of mustered seed and not by its size: "...*if ye have faith as a grain of mustered seed...*" (Luke 17:6). It is a vital nutrient, which helps control the balance of life within the body. The *Word of God* in like manner does the same: The balance of our faith in God depends on our knowledge factor of Him.

Knowledge is power under any circumstances, even in the life of faith. Only a few men have defeated great armies through their knowledge factors–secular, political, and/or spiritual. Read the biography of Sir. Winston Churchill and the tactics of wisdom he used during WW2 to defeat Hitler's assaults on his country. Read also in the Old Testament of the heroes of faith who defeated their enemies with no more than a jawbone of an ass (Judges 15:16).

To identify exactly what God is, man's power of comprehension has gone blank. We do know that *He is a Spirit*– but what is a spirit? We know also that the spirits He has created are likened unto His Spirit–in knowledge and in power, but with restrictions. We also have reason to believe that the spirits God created are likened unto man's spirit, because after the death of the body man's spirit returns to God who gave it (Eccl 12:7). We would think that when a man is possessed with an evil spirit it would inhabit his entire body, as some people appear to have demons in different parts of their body. There were thousands of evil spirits controlling his life and body (Luke 8:26-33) but it took only One Spirit to cast them all out. Reason: They were all home-based and operative in his mind. Even a pea-brain can house thousands of evil spirits in his mind, and by the same token, a pea-brain Christian with a grain of faith can cast them all out.

Satan was one of the most beautiful and powerful spirits of God's heavenly creation, but he let all his beauty and power go to his head and he lost his fellowship card. He was then disbanded from power and removed from the heavenly sphere to a lower state of service where he developed a trade in tempting man to disobey God (Ezek 28:13-19). As the result of this thought a worthy question has emerged: How could a spirit be beautiful if they are bodiless and invisible? Answer: Through thought characterization–humans are only as beautiful as their character. What may appear beautiful to the eyes of the beholder (such as a beautiful woman or a masculine man) is only a stack of cosmic physics generated by genetic composites held together by skin and bones. The beauty of all humanity dwells within their characterization factors and not their physical profile. (This is why marriage should be approached through character examination rather than from an outward point of view–the heart depends on the mind and the mind depends on the eyes–but since love is blind, character examination is the answer.)

Evil spirits are evil thoughts that continually challenge man's inquisitive mind with evil rhetoric, which then tempts man to sin. This is why I say that spirits are like thoughts;[5] their main entrances into our lives are through the same sense factors as the gospel, as *"Faith cometh by hearing..."* (Rom 10:17) *"And as a man thinketh in his heart, so is he..."* and so dwells God (Pro 23:7).

But is God like the wind that moves around and over the earth? Is He like the air we breathe? Though the *Spirit of God* is spoken of *"...as of a rushing mighty wind..."* (Acts 2:2) it only relates to the sound and not the Spirit's substance or Essence. God cannot be measured by the wind nor likened in substance: The wind has its own substance, so thus, we cannot say or believe that God is made up of suchlike. We cannot say that He is like a cloud because, like the wind, they too have their own substance. Likewise, smoke and fire and water and vapor, and/or whatever elements we attribute to God; none can be equated to His Essence. *God is a Spirit,* and that Spirit was made flesh with the help of a virgin girl that lived here on earth. And that Spirit that was *made flesh,* lived, walked and talked among men in a fleshly body for thirty-three and one/half years. That body then died and arose again in the same form but in a new fashion.

Then that new fashion walked and talked and ate food just as man until the day it was taken up into the heavens. And now that fashion of a body will forever be the point of contact concerning God. But not only so: We now have a God with a Body and He is now sitting upon the throne of David in Heaven just as it was promised, (2 Samuel 7:12-16, Acts 2:29-33)-(A.W. Pink).[4] Imagine that–God now has a body: A body that came up through the medium of human birth, with arms and legs and hands and feet and eyes and ears, and a heart, within which dwells all the fullness of the Godhead–and it is in bodily form, (Col 2:9) ruling and reigning as a Spirit within the heart and mind of men and women all across the world.

A note of interest: There are pastors who minister without logical connection: They lack orderly continuity with their congregations, so they rule by rubrics (standards of performance) that have turned stale through their own incoherency. They will inherit a robotic church, which functions under a mechanical theory that will eventually come unplugged, and believe me, I have seen many churches with pastors who are not plugged in. Now we can write about His Body.

Chapter 13

His Body

(Portions of this chapter is offered to us by the early church father, St John Chrysostom 346-406 AD, Volume XXV, Homily XXIV, Scriptures: (1 Cor 10:13), P190-198, PDF file. Copyright (1909) Public Domain (Italics added).[10]

I have placed this chapter *"His Body"* just before the chapter *"The Word Made Flesh"* to give the reader a better understanding of how the *"Word was made flesh,"* which was somewhat different in power, supremacy, and equality from man's body. We preach that the *"Word was made of flesh"* and we preach also that the *Spirit of God* was placed within that *Body* without measure or limitations. But if you read it right, it does not offer that thought. *"The Word was made flesh"* <u>throughout</u>, which means: every part of His body was made flesh by or from the *Word*–there were no foreign substances. Man was made of the same live-giving essence but was later given eternal Essence when God breathed into him the breath of life, and the pattern still exist today–but not so with God. His Essence was never temporal but was eternal. However, man's essence is a temporary loan form the Essence of God and must be returned upon the death of the body. The *Word* being *made flesh* did not compromise the Deity of God's Essence or man's temporal essence, but rather, was made sure through the sacrifice of Himself on the Cross. Students of the scripture must realize that the Essence of God (the *Word* of God) was made flesh as a seed is made after its kind. The contribution of the womb was its incubator and moisture chamber, from which it amalgamated (made the switch) into a human being.

This subject has been quite a controversy concerning *Jesus' Body*, as to whether or not it was human or divine or both. My research on this subject is on this wise: The quality of the flesh was the same but the *Essence* within was different in measure: An individual who has God in his heart has the same *essence* throughout; however, it is given unto man by measure. The quality of the Essence of the Holy Spirit within our lives is predicated upon the quality of the gospel we hear (1 Cor 3:10-15).

The gospel is designed to increase the Essence of God within man's lives, but man has turned to demonstration instead of consecration. *Jesus' Body* was divine in Essence but human in nature: It came to us undefiled and pure just as Adam's body came undefiled and pure. Adam's body was created from dust; Jesus' body was made of a woman. Adam's body was made of mortal (earthly) substances; immortality was added when God breathed into him the breath of life. The seed of death was not within Adam's body at his creation; death came as the result of sin. Jesus' Body was made from different properties and the seed of death was not within *His Body*. Adam was made of the earth–earthly; *Jesus* was conceived of heaven, pure, uncontaminated and sinless: created in our likeness and of our substance but under the decree of a new creation (Rev 3:14).

His Body could not die. *His Body* could not see corruption (decompose in the grave–was not possible that death could hold eternal life captive)[6] (Acts 13:35). *His Body* walked on water. *His body* turned water into wine. *His Body* healed the sick. *His body* turned fish and bread into an abundance. *His Body* rebuked demons and cast them out. *His Body* commanded the wind and waves to obey. From *His Body* came forth healing and eternal life. *His Body* possessed the precious blood of the New Covenant. Within *His Body* was God.

On the other hand: *His Body* became tired, weak, sleepy, and hungry. *His Body* required and suffered from all the same elements and fundamentals as man's body. *His Body* was so mysterious that not even the angels in heaven nor the apostles on earth could understand it. *His Body* suffered under the same laws of creation. *His Body*, though full of the Essence of God, died; yet *His body* came back to life. *His Body* then took on a new characteristic: *His Body* suddenly appeared to the disciples on the road to Emmaus, where *His Body* ate food and then *His Body*, including the food, vanished. *His Body* ascended up into the heavens. And through it all, *His Body* remained manifest and touchable.

O dear friend, dear reader, dear Christian student, *His Body* not only was the *"Lamb of God"* but *His Body* became also the *Throne of God*.

To continue our study of *"HIS BODY"* we turn now to the writings of St John Chrysostom. Quote:

"Very persuasively spake he, and awfully. For what he says is this: "This which is in the cup is that which flowed from His side, and of that do we partake." But he called it a cup of blessing, because holding it in our hands, we so exalt Him in our hymn, wondering, astonished at His unspeakable gift, blessing Him, among other things, for the pouring out of this self-same draught that we might not abide in error: and not only for the pouring it out, but also for the imparting thereof to us all. Wherefore if thou desire blood, saith He, redden not the altar of idols with the slaughter of brute beasts, but My altar with My blood."...Christ even herein exhibited His care and fervent love for us. And in the Old Covenant, because they were in an imperfect state, the blood which they used to offer to idols He Himself submitted to receive, that He might separate them from those idols; which very thing again was a proof of His unspeakable affection: but here He transferred the service to that which is far more awful and glorious, changing the very sacrifice itself, and instead of the slaughter of rational creatures, commanding to offer up Himself.

The bread which we break, is it not a communion of the *Body of Christ*?" Wherefore said he not, the participation? Because he intended to express something more and to point out how close was the union, in that, we communicate, not only by participating and partaking, but also by being united. For as that body is united to Christ so also are we united to him by this bread (*His Body*). But why, adds he also, "...*which we break*?" For although in the Eucharist one may see this done, yet on the cross not so, but the very contrary. For, "*A bone of Him*," saith one "*shall not be broken*." But that which He suffered not on the cross, this He suffers in the oblation for thy sake, and submits to be broken...which communicates another thing from that whereof...which seemeth to be but a small difference...For having said, "*A communion of the Body*," he sought again to express something nearer. Wherefore also, he added, "*For we, who are many, are one bread, one body*" (v-17).

"*For why speak I of communion?*" saith he, "We are that self-same body." For what is the bread? *The Body of Christ*. And what do they become who partake of it? *The Body of Christ*: Not many bodies, but one body. For as the bread consisting of many grains is made one, so that the grains nowhere appear; they exist indeed, but their difference is not seen by reason of their conjunction; so are we conjoined both with each other and with Christ: there not being one body for thee, and another for thy neighbor...but the very same for all. Wherefore also, he adds, "*For we all partake of the one bread*." Now if we are all nourished of the same and all become the same, why do we not also show forth the same love, and in this respect, one? For fallen from our eternal life we were exiles from the Paradise of delight, (St. John Chrysostom: Homilies on the Epistles of St Paul.)

Chrysostom to the Corinthians: This was the old way too in the time of our forefathers: "...*for the multitude of them that believed,"* saith the text *"were of one heart and soul,"* (Acts 4:32). Not so, however, now, but altogether the reverse. Many and various are the contests betwixt all, and worse than wild beasts are we affected towards each other's members…For he gave not simply even *His own Body*; but because the former nature of the flesh which was framed out of earth, had first become deadened by sin and destitute of life; He brought in, as one may say, another sort of dough and leaven, *His own flesh*, by nature indeed the same, but free from sin and full of life; and gave to all to partake thereof, that being nourished by this and laying aside the old dead material, we might be blended together unto that which is living and eternal, by means of this table.

"Behold Israel after the flesh: have not they which eat the sacrifices communion with the altar?" (V-18).

Again, from the Old Covenant he leads them unto this point also…it is *"a Communion of the Lord's Body."* For not with the altar, but with *Christ Himself*, do we have communion…Do not then run to the contrary things. For neither if thou wert a king's son, and having the privilege of thy father's table, should leave it and choose to partake of the table of the condemned and the prisoners in the dungeon, would thy father permit it, but with great vehemence he would withdraw thee; not as though the table could harm thee, but because it disgraces thy nobility and the royal table…*Perceivest thou the kindness of a careful father?*

These things therefore knowing, let us also, beloved, consult for the good of the brethren and preserve unity with them. For to this that fearful and tremendous sacrifice leads us, warning us above all things to approach it with one mind and fervent love, and thereby becoming eagles, so to mount up to the very heaven, nay, even beyond the heaven. *"For wheresoever the carcass is, saith He, there also will be the eagles"* (Matt 24:28). Calling *His body* a carcass by reason of *His death*, for unless He had fallen we should not have risen again. But He calls us eagles, implying that he who draws nigh to this *Body* must be on high and have nothing common with the earth...but must ever be soaring heavenwards...For eagles, not dogs, have a right to this table...what shall we say of the *Body of Him Who is God over all*, spotless, pure, associate with the Divine Nature, the *Body* whereby we are, and live; "This Table is not, saith Chrysostom, for chattering jays, (blue jays) but for eagles, who fly thither where the dead *Body* lieth."

The souls of the righteous are compared unto eagles, because they seek what is on high...If then we have come to know what the eagles are, we can no longer doubt about the *Body*; especially if we recollect that *Body* which Joseph once received from Pilate. Seem they not unto thee as eagles around a *Body*, I mean, Mary, the wife of Cleopas, and Mary Magdelene, and Mary the Mother of the Lord, and the gathering of the Apostles around the Lord's entombing? Doth it not seem to thee as eagles around a *Body*, when the Son of Man shall come with the mystical clouds, and every eye shall see Him, and they also, which pierced Him?

There is also the *Body* concerning which it was said, "*My Flesh is meat indeed, and My Blood is drink indeed.*" Around this *Body* are certain eagles, which hover over it with spiritual wings. They are also eagles round the *Body*, which believe that *Jesus is come in the Flesh*: since "*Every spirit which confesseth that Jesus Christ is come in the flesh, is of God.*" Wheresoever then faith is, there is the Sacrament, and there, the resting place of holiness. Again, *this Body is the Church*, wherein by the grace of *Baptism* we are renovated in spirit, and whatever tends to decay through old age is refreshed, for ages of new life."

Let us not slay ourselves by our irreverence, but with all awfulness and purity draw nigh to it; and when thou see it set before thee, say thou to thyself, "Because of this *Body* am I no longer a prisoner but free...this *Body*, nailed and scourged, was more than death could stand against; this *Body* the very sun saw sacrificed, and turned aside his beams; for this both the veil was rent in that moment, and rocks burst asunder, and all earth was shaken. This is even that *Body*, the blood-stained, the pierced, that out of which gushed the saving fountains, the one of blood, the other of water, for all the world." Would thou from another source also learn its power? Ask of her diseased with an issue of blood, who laid hold, not of the *Body*, but of the garment with which it was clad. Ask of the sea, which bare the *Body* on its back. Ask even of the Devil himself, and say, "Whence hast thou that incurable stroke? Whence hast thou no longer any power? Whence art thou captive? By whom hast thou been seized in thy flight?" And he will give no other answer than this: "The *Body* that was crucified." Ask also Death, and say, "Whence is it that thy sting hath been taken away? Thy victory abolished? Thy sinews cut out? And thou become the laughing-stock of girls and children, who was before a terror even to kings and to all righteous men?" And he will ascribe it to this *Body*. For when this *Body* was crucified, then were the dead raised up, then was that prison burst, and the gates of brass were broken, and the dead were loosed and the keepers of hell-gate all covered in fear...death on the contrary should have become more mighty; but it was not so...therefore was death dissolved?

This *Body* hath He given to us both to hold and to eat a thing appropriate to intense love...Job said, "*Oh! That we were filled with his flesh!*" (Job 31:31). Even so, Christ hath given to us to be filled with His flesh, drawing us on to greater love.

Let us draw nigh to Him then with fervency and with inflamed love, that we may not have to endure punishment. For in proportion to the greatness of the benefits bestowed on us, so much the more exceedingly are we chastised when we show ourselves unworthy of the bountifulness. This *Body*, even lying in a manger, reverenced. Yea, men profane and barbarous, leaving their country and their home, both set out on a long journey, and when they came, with fear and great trembling worshipped Him. Let us, then, at least imitate those Barbarians, we who are citizens of heaven. For they indeed when they saw Him but in a manger, drew nigh with great awe; but thou behold Him not in the manger but on the altar, not a woman holding Him in her arms, but the priest standing by, and the Spirit with exceeding bounty hovering over the gifts set before us. Thou do not see merely this *Body* itself as they did, but know also its power, and the whole economy, and art ignorant of none of the holy things, which are brought to pass by it, having been exactly initiated into all. Let us therefore rouse ourselves up and be filled with horror, and let us show forth a reverence far beyond that of those Barbarians; that we may not, by random and careless approaches heap fire upon our own heads.

But these things I say, not to keep us from approaching, but to keep us from approaching without consideration. For as the approaching at random is dangerous, so the not communicating in those mystical suppers is famine and death. For this *Table* is the sinews of our soul, the bond of our mind, and the foundation of our confidence, our hope, our salvation, our light, and our life. When with this sacrifice we depart into the outer world, with much confidence we shall tread the sacred threshold, fenced round on every side as with a kind of golden armor. And why speak I of the world to come? Since here this mystery makes earth become to thee a heaven. Open only for once the gates of heaven and look in; nay, rather not of heaven, but of the heaven of heavens; and then thou wilt behold what I have been speaking of. For what is there most precious of all, this will I show thee lying upon the earth. For as in royal palaces, what is most glorious of all is not walls, nor golden roofs, but the person of the king sitting on the throne; so likewise in heaven the *Body of the King*. But this, thou art now permitted to see upon earth. For it is not angels, nor archangels, nor heavens and heavens of heavens, that I show thee, but the very Lord and Owner of these. Perceive thou how that which is more precious than all things is seen by thee on earth; and not seen only, but also touched; and not only touched, but likewise eaten; and after receiving it thou go home? Make thy soul clean then; prepare thy mind for the reception of these mysteries. For if entrusted to carry a king's child with the robes, the purple, and the diadem, would cast away all things which are upon the earth. But now that it is no child of man how royal so ever, but the only-begotten Son of God Himself, Whom thou received; do thou not thrill with awe, tell me, and cast away all the love of all worldly things, and have no bravery but that wherewith to adorn thyself? Or do thou still look towards earth, and love money, and pant after gold? What pardon then can thou have? What excuse? Knowest thou not that all this worldly luxury is loathsome to thy Lord? Was it not for this that on His birth He was laid in a manger, and took to Himself a mother of low estate? Did He not for this say to him that was looking after gain, *"But the Son of Man hath not where to lay His head"* (Matt. 8:20).

St. John Chrysostom: (Homilies on the Epistles of Paul to the Corinthians: And what did the disciples? Did they not observe the same law, being taken to houses of the poor and lodged, one with a tanner, another with a tent-maker, and with the seller of purple: For they inquired not after the splendor of the house but for the virtues of men's souls. These therefore let us also emulate, hastening by the beauty of pillars and of marbles, and seeking the mansions, which are above; and let us tread under foot all the pride here below with all love of money, and acquire a lofty mind. For if we be sober-minded, not even this whole world is worthy of porticoes, (covered walkways) much less arcades (arches and columns) and us. Wherefore, I beseech you; let us adorn our souls, let us fit up this House, which we are also to have with us when we depart; that we may attain even to the eternal blessings, through the grace and mercy of God–*"His Body."* Unquote.[10]

Chapter 14

The Word Was Made Flesh

There was something strange about this man called Jesus that attracted the Apostle John's attention. John's education placed him in front of the line in understanding the Old Testament writings, which predicated his knowledge of Jesus' strange birth: His deity, His manhood, how did it happen, who was He, and why did He come into the world. Thus, it would be John who would reveal Jesus' true identity as the *Word Made Flesh*.

Christians and ministers all across our world, especially among the Oneness Pentecostal ministries, who want to hypothesize on (John 1:14) in their preaching need to re-read the structure of this scripture again: Their speculation of words express plainly that they do not understand what John was writing about when he wrote, *"…the word was made flesh."* A most popular pet-pea among global-theologians of all religions is the expression: *"…the word become flesh."* (The Word did *not become* flesh.) I would like to remind Bible students and seasoned ministers to quote this scripture *"as it is written."* Because, changing just one *"jot or tittle"* can also change the thought behind the expression. If the *Word became flesh*, we could then concede that Jesus preexisted as a separate entity within the godhead with the Father in eternity; but that is a contradiction of the first commandment: *"Hear O Israel: The LORD our GOD is ONE LORD"* (Duet 6:4).

The word *made*, in this verse, is a *transitive verb*, which surrenders its flash of fame to the dominant verb–*dwelt*, as in *"dwelt among us."* The power and the glory within this verse lies, not in the transitive verb, *made,* but in the dominant verb–*dwelt,* which means: There are more mysteries hidden in God *dwelling* among us than Him being *made* flesh. God came into the world–that is not a mystery; however, Him dwelling among us–that is a mystery. The *Word* could not be *made flesh* in heaven but only here on earth. God could love us from heaven, but His love could not be made manifest to us in its fullness unless He dwelt among us; He could not be made a sin offering for us in heaven, it had to be expressed here on earth through the flesh.[4]

When something becomes something else it loses its first identity and/or ceases to exist in its originality–its original essence. The *Word* did not *become* flesh. Jesus did not become God–He was God, and He was *made* flesh for the purpose of becoming a human sacrifice for sin. But how was *the Word* made flesh? We assume that Jesus' Body received its flesh from Mary through her ability to produce children. But remember: Jesus was the seed of a new creation–fashioned in the same manner as man. Just as an acorn has everything it needs to produce itself into a tree, *including the bark,* even so did the Word of God. Could it be that Mary's only contribution was the incubation of the seed? St. John Chrysostom called *His Body* a new type of flesh–a new type of leaven (P-93-L-9-11). But would this remove His existence as a real human being? Since seeds need dirt for warmth and moisture to start the process of being *made* into a tree, likewise the *Word* seed needed the same to initiate the amalgamation process of being made into a baby.

As I wrote earlier: *God is a Spirit* and since spirits have no substance, (cosmic physics as man) and since thoughts must first be made into a substance before they can physically exist, God's thoughts must first be made into human flesh before they could be physically known. I noticed the phrase: *(overshadow)* in (Luke 1:35) and how it is used with the word *conceived.* The word *overshadow* is also transitive in its nature and is pointing to the dominant verb, *born,* which we are writing about.

The student will be wise to examine their desired subjects from every perspective within the Holy Scriptures. Since sex between a male and a female is the common manner of conception, this is why the scribe used the word *"overshadow"* as in, to *overlay* or to lay-upon. However, medical science has come up with other methods of conception, which was unknown to the holy scribes. But since this conception was without human sperm cells, what type of conception was it? The mystery of this conception was on this wise: Spirits are <u>NOT</u> procreant; (procreative) they do not and are not capable of reproducing. So, then, where did the sperm cells come from and what type were they? Answer: The *Word* was the sperm: The Spirit of God entered into Mary's womb and introduced a new type of sperm. You say, "God cannot do that–this is a contradiction to what you are saying."

Let me remind the student that God is God and God can do as God pleases, however, whenever and to whomever. It was an act of Spirit insemination; an act of deliberate introduction of sperm cells. God created the law of birth and He, by His own will, became a subject of His own law. If God can make a body from dust, introducing a new creation through a virgin birth was a breeze. His *Word* was *made* into a human cell and found its way into the virgin womb and the creation of God into our likeness began; this is what John was trying to tell us in this one verse (St. John 1:14).

But there is this question: Was it a human sperm cell, a Spirit sperm cell, or was it a new type of sperm cell? Answer: His *Word* was His *sperm,* which brought forth God's new creation. Jesus was the beginning of a new creation, and this is why *His Body* was such a mystery to all who knew Him–as we have previously written concerning *His Body*. Some theologians believe Jesus' *Body* was totally human, whereas others believe it was totally divine. And then there are those who believe it was both human and divine. Whichever, whatever, or however,

His body was accepted as the sacrifice for the sins of the world–mystery solved.

Many writers have written that the Holy Spirit had sexual intercourse with Mary and thus, she conceived thereby and had a child. They do not know what they are writing about and will one day regret their foolishness. God had to have a human body as a substance to become a human sacrifice. And since spirits cannot reproduce, God's thoughts were used as the Essence of His substance, which produced a new type of sperm and it entered into Mary's womb and the *"Word was made flesh."*

Our Lord was the beginning of a new creation: Made under the same law and through the same process as man. However, being conceived by the *Holy Ghost*, the seed of sin and death was not in Him: By virtue of Him being God He could not die, but being a man however, He could die. Thus, giving His life as a ransom for everyone who would believe in Him, He did die. Do you believe in Him?

Being *made* flesh was God's way of making His entrance into our world. He did it through the same expression as man; through the form of a *son*, and this is how we got the expression *"The Son of God."* God pulled off a great scheme by disguising Himself as a son and the devil never knew that Jesus was God in the flesh until after he had put Him to death–in the flesh. Satan did not carnage His Essence but His substance. And this is the mystery that is still hidden from the heart and mind of those who appose the Deity of Jesus Christ; Him being God and man at the same time is still a mystery to the world. So, then, the phrase *"...that which is conceived in her"* is God's way of expressing His plan in our language and on our level of intellectual reasoning so the devil would think likewise.

"Thoughts are only valuable in proportion to the wisdom of those who transpose them into lyrics, which gives rise to feelings and dreams. David wrote in his Psalm: *"How precious are thy thoughts unto me, O Lord"* (Ps 143:17). But to give these thoughts to us, God must first clothe them in a language within reach of our comprehension; which means: He clothed His thoughts in flesh to express to us His passions of love.

As one great writer expressed it: "Actions were first thoughts, (Matt 15:19) that must first be clothed with a body of some form in order to be made known...Jesus Christ was the *Word of God*: He was the revelation of the Father's thoughts to the world, which was clothed with flesh." R.C. Trench.[12]

"He that winneth souls is wise" because he clothes his words with transcending wisdom: He presents God to man in garments of familiarity and in languages sinners can understand.

Remember these familiarities? He clothed His thoughts in a burning bush to speak to Moses, (Ex 3:2-5). He clothed His thoughts in the form of a dumb ass to speak to Balaam, (2 Peter 2:16). He again clothed His thoughts in the form of a fish to speak to Jonah, (Jonah 1:17). He also clothed His thoughts as the brightness of the sun to speak to Saul, who later became known as the Apostle Paul (Acts 9:3). Sometimes it's not what is said that gets the attention but how it is said, and God has a way of saying it the right way.

Anthropomorphic or *Anthropomorphism* (n) is an expression that is used to express a condescending message from a King to a beggar: From a resident to a foreigner, from God to man, from someone who knows and understands to someone who does not know or understand: As from a parent to child, a teacher to a student; it is especially effective within the world of elementary expressions. Comparing that which is higher in understanding to that which is lower in knowledge. Which means: "The attribution of a human form with human characteristics, or human behavior, to nonhuman things, such as deities in mythology and animals in children's stories."[5]

Children, many times, have no idea of what the adult world is talking about until we sit down and tell the story to them in their language. Adults live in a lofty world of knowledge, whereas children live in an elementary world of animated imagery, and we adults have to find, define, and refine what we say to connect with their world. We have to create an animated image and transpose it into tiny fragments of faith as if it were real. This not only is true with children, it is also true with unbelievers as well as many Christians. People who have not yet experienced the new birth of the Spirit have no concept of spiritual imagery; thus, Christian teachers must find an avenue of thought comprehensible to their level of thinking.

God lives in a celestial sphere with angels that are able to appear in the form of a *metamorphosis expression* as though they were human beings. However, man cannot do that, because man is confined and limited to this world. God's dwelling place is far above our entitlement of understanding, and the expressions used therein are beyond our ability to decode. Therefore, *His Holy Book*, the *Bible*, is mostly composed of, or is written in *anthropomorphic expressions* to help man break through the language barrier. Thus, God's thoughts were transposed into a language man is familiar with–simple factor, simple fact.

The expression of streets and other objects being in the glory world are only *anthropomorphic expressions* designed for our understanding. And besides, spirits have no need of such things because they are thoughts waiting to be expressed. The expression of food, as in (Ps 78:25) *"Man did eat angels food..."* is also another *anthropomorphic expression*, because spirits have no need of food; they are not subject too nor do they depend upon natural nutrition to survive. Angel food is the same as Christian's food; their nourishment too is the *Word of God*.

The marriage supper of the Lamb is another transcending expression concerning food. What the marriage supper will consist of I cannot tell; however, since the spirit world is independent from human necessities, it will be something that this world has never seen or could imagine; thus it is described as such on man's level as a hypothesis–a hint (1 Cor 2:9-11). What things are revealed to our spirits is mystical and not tangible. The feelings in that world will not be according to the rule of human nature as here on earth, and neither will our new celestial bodies be subject to our former limitations, qualities, infirmities or dependences.

Anthropomorphic expressions are used throughout the Holy Scriptures when relating stories because they improve the understanding factors within the scenarios. But because we are human beings, God must relate to the things we know and are familiar with so we will have some understanding of what things will be like in heaven–but on a celestial scale. A city, for instance, with walls of gasper, gates of pearl, and streets of gold, we earthlings can only imagine. However, spirits have no need of these things, because they are thoughts that minister to the heirs of salvation. Whatever heaven's reality man cannot imagine; however, it is expressed as thus as a model for thought.

Another short example of an *anthropomorphic expression*: *"And the lord God formed man of the dust of the ground, and breathed into his nostrils the breath of life; and man became a living soul"* (Gen 2:7). There is a glitch within this scripture that most students fail to see: *Spirits do not breathe*; they are not subject to nor do they depend upon oxygen. Creatures that breathe are subject to fatigue, exhaustion, and death. However, neither God nor the angels are subject to any of these frailties or limitations. Spirits are like thoughts: They never tire, they never grow old or wear-out; they never sleep and neither do they die. Though the Bible speaks of God resting on the Seventh or Sabbath Day and falling asleep on a boat, (Gen 2:2, Matt 8:24, 25). We cannot take sleeping and resting at face value. These are *anthropomorphic expressions* designed for man's level of thinking. The Omnipotent sovereignty of God synchronized everything in the beginning to be self-sovereign.

So, again, what is the writer of (Genesis 2:7) trying to tell us concerning God breathing, as though He was subject to our necessities, rationalities, limitations and/or timeframes? He is above and beyond any and all earthly forces that we are subject or restricted too–we cannot rationalize God.

The preposition within this story is to bring man from spiritual darkness into His marvelous light: *God is* still *a Spirit* and the gospel is His *sperm*, and sons and daughters are being born again all over the world. His new creation of Himself has placed Him on the throne of David as a man. His new body is His right hand, and His sitting down is His finished work of redemption. His ascension created a ladder wherewith man may ascend and descend before His throne through prayer. His eyes before and behind are an expression of His universal love. His Essence is the voice of the gospel, which we preach and man believes–why not believe today–this is the meaning behind these *anthropomorphic expressions.*

Chapter 15

A Paradox Of Incoherency

Some Bible scholars believe that God created Adam by mixing dust like a potter then breathed into his nostrils and he started breathing. Others believe God created Adam's body from the dust of the ground and then placed into it a spirit; and thus, man became a *humanoid*–a living human being with a spirit. And then there are those who believe that God brea*thed* into Adam's nostrils and he sat up and said, cool, got up, stretched, and said, let's get started. I think these theories are a little far out. I cannot agree to either theory because of the timeframe of their expression and the style of the verbs: *"And the Lord God formed man of the dust of the ground, and breathed into his nostrils the breath of life; and man became a living soul"* (Gen 2:7).

Though we do not understand completely how this transpired yet we must accept it *as it is written*. But, because it is written: *"...man became a living soul."* Are we to believe that Adam's soul was first dead and then made alive, or was this the final touch in God creating him–was man created in phases? Was it the soul that made him alive, was it the spirit that made him alive, or was it the breath of life that made him alive? At what time did God place into Adam a spirit and a soul? Was it a body that was dead and waiting for a spirit, was it a body with a spirit that was waiting to be made alive, or was it the combination of all the above? We know what part the body plays in our existence; but what part then does the spirit and soul play in our existence? We know that at some point God put life into Adam. But why the expression "...*man became a living soul?*" Why not "Adam was *made* a living soul?" After all, he had just come into existence. The moment God created the seed of man (Adam) his life began; he had to be alive, life was within the seed–the essence. But why the addition of "...*the breath of life?*" When God made Adam, He made him of or from His own Essence; and thus, life came with his creation.

Something that becomes something else must already exist; you do not become something else unless you are already something. The caterpillar was doing fine as he was *made*, but his life really changed when he *became* a butterfly; but it happened by virtue of his already being alive. And when it *became* a butterfly, it left behind the old creation of itself and took on a new creation filled with new adventures.

This is the way it's supposed to be when man is born again: His life will change and he will *become* "*a new creature in Christ Jesus*" (2 Cor 5:17). And with the change will also come new experiences and adventures. It is this author's belief that when God *breathed* into Adam's nostrils, He added something to Adam's life that made him alive to himself and to God–but what was that something? Adam was already alive and well, breathing, walking, talking and looking things over. He had to be already alive because he was the seed of man, and being the seed of man, life and everything else came with the body.

Life was within the seed of Adam's creation–he was a pure man. As A.W. Pink wrote: "Behind him was no sinful heredity, within him was no deceitful and wicked heart, upon him were no marks of corruption, and around him were no signs of death."[4] Though not yet alive to the knowledge and existence of God: His eyes were open only to the things surrounding his world. Being alive but disconnected is a paradox of incoherency and Adam was the first example.

This is a great lesson concerning the life of sinners who are alive but not yet conscious of God; Adam's eyes were only open to the things around him but not to the things of God. Just as Adam was not yet aware of God, so also are sinners: They walk, talk, and are alive, but they are not conscious of God–I know I wasn't. So what is the writer of (Genesis 2:7) trying to tell us since God does not breathe? (I am by no means saying that God cannot breathe, only that He is not subject to oxygen.)

Adam was made a mortal being; he was alive to his world but yet dead to the things of God. The Apostle Paul offers to us a great example concerning being dead while being alive. *"But she that liveth in pleasure is dead while she liveth"* (1 Tim 5:6). This person was both alive and dead at the same time; she was alive to the things of this world but dead to the things of God. Another example is found in the book of Acts, where Paul and Silas were speaking to a group of women by a river, of which it is said concerning a girl named Lydia *"…whose heart the Lord opened"* (Acts 16:14).

I can relate to this. I can remember back over the years to the time that I was alive and well but dead to the things of God, until someone told me about Jesus Christ. I was alive and having a good time in the world around me, but I was disconnected from God. I was breathing air and eating food, I had blood flowing through my veins and life was going on. But like Lydia, who was disconnected form God until she heard Paul speaking words of eternal life. After I heard the things concerning the kingdom of God and the way of righteousness, my heart was suddenly opened and my soul *became* alive to the things of God–I got connected to heaven's Wi-Fi–how about you?

Adam was alive and doing well in his little world of attending the garden and musing himself on the opportunities of what he saw. But he was not alive to God or the things of God; he was as dead to God as any sinner is dead to God today. When we read the expression that *"God breathed into his nostrils the breath of life and man became a living soul;"* this is a *before* and *after* story" of how Adam got connected with God. His body was alive, his spirit was alive, but in his mind and heart he was not alive–I remember those days–do you?

Breath and *spirit* are synonymous in their nature and meaning; they are interchangeable. Whether He breathed or poured out His Spirit the meaning is the same. The word *Breathed* is a transitive verb and is used to instill a particular quality into a subject or object, somebody, or some thing. It can be a way of speaking, but with God it can be through a mule, a fish, or a bush: The coach *breathed* new life into the group of players during the sports break and they won the game. Or, as in war, when soldiers are being prepped to face deadly situations: The drill sergeant *breathes* into them a fighting spirit by means of a pep talk. Likewise, with supervisors who want more production from their employees: They *breathe* into them an aggressive spirit to get more production.

A transitive verb is a word that has relationship to or describes the dominant verb, i.e. *"And Saul, yet breathing out threatenings and slaughter against the disciples of the Lord"* (Acts 9:1). He did not kill them with his breath, (thought some people could) but in his righteous indignation of breathing out threats of slaughter, they were overpowered in their spirits and became the same as dead men. The *transitive* verb is *breathing*, but the *dominant* verb is *slaughter*, which when they heard, it literally subdued them. Don't tell me you have never been overcome by fear when someone threatened you.

The writer of (Genesis 2:7) used a transitive verb to attract the reader's interest to examine the life of Adam. Sinners, when they hear and accept the preaching of the gospel, they become a living soul–alive to God. God had to turn Adam's lights on in his soul before he could spiritually see the reality of God. The scripture in (Gen 2:7) does <u>not</u> read, "Adam became a living soul" as so often quoted. It reads as thus: "...*and man became a living soul.*" The reference here is a prerequisite qualifying of requirement, not for Adam only, but for all who would believe in God in the future ages–a shadow of things to come.

Adam is here used as a decisive factor and example for all mankind. The scripture in (1 Cor 15:45) *"The first man Adam..."* is not the story of Adam's creation, but a comparison of flesh to Spirit: From the first man–Adam, to the second man–Christ Jesus, and to all who after would believe. Adam received his soul when he was created; however, it *became* a living soul (a responsive soul) when God breathed into him the *breath of life*–this is only an expression. This is how and why we have so many people walking around today who are dead within their souls; they are alive in the body but dead in their spirit. Let me say this again: They are asleep in heart and dead in mind. However, when God *breathes* into them through the *voice* of the gospel, their hearts are awakened and their mind becomes aware of the presence and reality of God. Adam was first made a mortal (earthly) being, then, when God *breathed* into him the *breath of life*, his heart was opened and immortality (eternal life) was added to his life. This *breath of life* is different from just breathing air; it has eternal life within it. Sinners have life, but they receive eternal life when they believe and obey the *gospel*. And it is still happening today within the lives of people all over the world who have believed and obeyed the gospel.

Though I said, *"God does not breathe"*(v). God's breath is the *voice* of the gospel ministered through the *breath* of the ministry. Though our modern theologians deny the fact of the old fashion infilling of the *Holy Ghost* with speaking in or with tongues, yet people are receiving it today and are becoming living souls, conscious of God. Adam did not know God until He breathed into him the breath of life, and that same *breath* is the gospel. The *Word of God*, (the gospel) is still *breathing* life into millions today. When people receive the Holy Ghost, it is God breathing into them the breath of life.

The words *Theophany* or *Theophanic* are expressions of manifestations: "Man is a Tripartite being: he is made up of spirit, soul, and body, (1 Thess 5:23). The late Dr. Pierson distinguished them as thus: "The spirit as *God-consciousness*, the soul as the seat of *self-consciousness,* and the body as *sense-consciousness.*"⁽⁴⁾ As sinners we were *self-conscious* but not *God-conscious*–God was not yet enthroned within our hearts. That's the way it was with Adam; he was self-conscious, but not God conscious: he became *God conscious* when God breathed into him the breath of life. But it was not until after he sinned did he become *sense conscious,* which made him aware of his lost condition. His eternal life was then revoked because of his sin–their sin. It is strange how sin becomes energized and magnified when we become *sense conscious* (Rom 7:7). I really didn't think about sin until I came in contact with eternal life; and then sin really became an issue.

In closing this chapter let me reiterate: The Old Testament is written in mystical mysteries and shadows, which all point to the New Testament time and era. What the Old Testament conceals in mysteries the New Testament reveals in revelations–each is a dictionary for the other.

Chapter 16

Emotional Ecstasy

We now will speak briefly again concerning (John 3:8) where Jesus is speaking to Nicodemus in relation to the new birth of the Spirit (John 3:1-12). Strange, how this scripture keeps popping up and falling into place in the line-up of thought. I am going to be downright critical concerning *bodily exercise* when it comes to worshipping God. True, there is some profit within the motion factor we display during our worship service, but can the profit factor be increased through intensified efforts or should the *Word of God* by the venerator that sets the standard? Is it God's Spirit shaking us or are we just shaking ourselves because it's the thing to do? Is it really the heavenly breeze we feel or is it our own wind-devil that is moving us; is it God's Spirit or our fancy?

Some Christians have told me that they just could not help what they were doing and that it was the *Holy Spirit* that had control of their emotions. Others have said they did it because others were doing it and thought it was the thing to do, and they felt out of place if they didn't do it. One brother said he did it because it was fun. Emotions are a strange part of our character that is controlled by music and other compelling forces, but some have coerced response of intimidations. There is also a lot of ministerial pressure that drives people to worship by imagination instead of consecration.

When King David recovered the Ark of the Covenant from the house of Obededom and was returning it to the city of Jerusalem, (2 Sam 6:14-16) the excitement of the moment was so amazing to David's thoughts that he burst forth in a dance before the Lord with all his might, and he danced so enthusiastically that his royal robs fell off. But through it all David was conscious of his actions because he was dancing as unto the Lord and this was his expression of praise. The joy of the moment had released an adrenalin factor of excitement because the Ark of God was returning to the nation. However, many people cut a rug and jitterbug without having any type of spiritual reasons. Though God is worthy of praise just by the fact of His redeeming us on Calvary, yet, there remains the fact that intellectual worship is more honorable than empty gymnastics, especially when there is no spiritual meaning behind it. Charles H. Spurgeon, the prince of preachers, noted it on this wise: "There should be more care for a grain of faith than a ton of excitement.[7]

There are some who say that David danced until all his clothes fell off his body, and he continued dancing naked before Lord and before all the people. This is an indication of a depraved mind that this man of God would expose himself and that before his people. David was *"...girded with a linen ephod"* over his clothing, and it was the royal linen ephod, which came loose and fell to the ground. It was not common for a king to remove his royal robes out in the public eye, especially during engagements with other kings or government activities. The only problem with David's ephod coming loose and falling to the ground was with his wife's opinion, who did not believe in getting undignified over the glory of God returning to Israel. And there are plenty of *Michal's* still with us yet today who despise this style or type of worship.

Whether a Prodigal is returning home to repent of his or her going astray, a Christian returning from their apostasy, or a sinner repenting before God; when the gospel is bringing home the gold there's nothing wrong with showing off emotional ecstasy. However, in the course of David's dancing before the

Lord, he was still in full control of his emotions. The Lord did not have control of his body as the unlearned exclaim: *"...the spirits of the prophets are subject to the prophets...For God is not the author of confusion, but of peace, as in all churches..."* (1 Cor 14:32-33).

Unrestrained and empty adulations (physical emotions) are the results of defectiveness within the ministry who controls their audience through excitements rather than by the *Word of God*. They create circumstances to display a show of their success, but in reality, it weakens the respect of their personal ministry. This was not David's problem. True worship is venerated by knowledge factors that promote righteousness, and if the *Word of God* is not the promoting factor, emotional ecstasy will come from the flesh and not from the Spirit of God. There are three characteristics of true worship: *Apprehension, Affection*, and *Expression*. There is a radical difference between natural hilarity and spiritual charity, and knowledge is the separating factor. Our experience with God is of a spiritual essence and not that of physical. Meaning: Pure devotion emancipates pure emotions.

Throughout the annals of scriptural characterization it was the trials and storms of life that established the true pattern of worship; after which, joy filled their hearts and they worshipped God in a dance as an expression of their gratitude. Worship is not controlled by our temperaments, but by the prevailing dominance within our experience of God and the quality of the *Word of God*; it is then naturalized through our fellowship with one another. When we loose control of our emotions we loose control of the will of God. Some worshipers act as if they were chasing shadows instead of having hold of the horns of the altar. Again: Charles H. Spurgeon, the prince of preachers, called it *"celestial convulsions."*[7]

The pastor of the Oneness Pentecostal Church in the city of Corinth thought he had the greatest church in the province, and so did its members. They had all the gifts, signs, wonders, and miracles within their services. However, their pride in their success gave birth to a crust of self-confidence that made them feel they were beyond reproach. But when the Apostle Paul came to visit, he was not impressed with their character or their nature of services. The news of their hypocritical disorder had quickly spread throughout the region, and not even the apostle Paul could suppress those who wanted to dominate the services through demeaning benevolence.

Do we dance before the Lord to show forth discreteness or discretion? All our shouting: All our running the isles, leaping, doing bullfrog hops and flip-flops, rolling in the floor, jumping up and down, waving our arms and hands. Do people really bring glory to God through these emotional gestures, or do they bring a reproach against the sovereignty of the *Holy Spirit*? Our excuse: "I like to be in the spirit when I worship the Lord." That's wonderful–so do I. And if you want to act in that fashion and call it worship, go ahead and chase the wind. But be aware, that any time you worship the Lord with your body, make sure it is regulated by precepts and fashions based upon the *written word*; otherwise, you could be offering up strange fire.

The Corinthian church was blessed with all the gifts of the Spirit; but they were also out of order to the respect that visitors thought they were mad, even to the extent that they nearly lost fellowship with God, (1 Cor, Ch 13 & 14). Just as faith needs substance to be motivated; even so, worship needs a substance to be genuine. Jesus spake of it on this wise: *"Ye worship ye know not what: We know what we worship for salvation is of the Jews"* (John 4:22). The church at Corinth was made up of Greek philosophers, orthodox Jews, and Gentile converts, and their principal problem as believers was, they lacked substance in their worship.

This is a lack of teaching within the ministry and leadership whose ability to minister is falling short of the true mark of stewardship, as true worship depends upon the *quality* of what is being ministered. Why else would the Apostle Paul have written such an insurrection against their leadership (1 Cor 1:10-17)? Any clergy can create a mechanical atmosphere with all the bells and whistles of excitement. However, sooner or later the hot air of emotional ecstasy will dissipate, leaving a congregation desperate for the *Word of God*, which could develop into a morbid epidemic of spiritual deficiency.

What composes these ecstatic desires to go beyond the true meaning of worship? If it is the hearing of the *Word of God* then let's keep it going full speed, because great preaching will put a dancing into your feet and a clapping to your hands like the sound of *"a rushing mighty wind."* Nothing so ignites a fire within a church service, as does the richness of the *Word of God*; it-uproots sin and renews health to the soul. Knowledge is as fuel to the fire of God's Spirit; it ignites emotional praises within the heart; but where there is no preaching, there is no fuel to ignite the fire.

Music has always been an igniter and/or a soother of emotions for the soul–but it has never at any time earned its sovereignty as a substitute for, or its superiority over the *spoken Word of God*. People go to sleep to the sound of smoothing music, and likewise, people wake up to the sound of motivating music; it can put you to sleep or it can set you on fire. When as a sinner I heard rock and roll music I went wild; whereas today, when I hear gospel music it's like drinking from the fountain of life.

Music reaches into the soul of man just as God's *Word* reaches into the soul of man; it turns him on or off–depending on the quality of both. But music should never become the core of our worship. If we offer to God a false display of ecstasy, we offer to Him a false display of worship. Let the *Word of God* be the igniting factor of worship and *"…let all things be done decently and in order"* (1 Cor 14:40).

According to this scripture, (John 3:8) it is the wind that blows first, and then we hear the sound thereof. True, God's Spirit moves in our services like as the wind. However, when

How Do Giants Fall?

His Spirit moves, it is because *His Word* is falling like manna from heaven, which motivates people to display an out of the ordinary devotion. God is in our mind as yeast is in dough, and like heat from fire, *His Word* brings rise to our emotions. When St. John said, *"I was in the Spirit on the Lord's day..."* (Rev 1:10) he simply meant he was in a transitive mood of devotion; His emotions were in tune with his devotions. But many people are motivated by tradition; they respond according to the order of the service. Acquaintance with the Most High God is the best factor to facilitate our jubilant expressions; without which, all else is self-fashioned.

Whether healings, songs, testimonies, or the fertility of the *Word of God*; during an out-pouring of the *Gift of the Holy Ghost* all seems to be accepted. However, not all we see is all of what we get within a runaway service. God's Spirit will never display itself in such a manner to deceive the audience and neither should the worshiper. A lot of our display is a trying to get under the spout where the Spirit is coming out, which is an operation of the flesh and not of the *Holy Spirit*. There is plenty *Holy Ghost* rain for all if all will wait upon the right cloud.

Chapter 17

Utterance Or Mutterance

This second chapter of the *Book of Acts* strengthens our subject concerning speaking in tongues. And I do enter into it with fear and trembling, lest I should create a misconception concerning the way God moves within and among His people, and neither do I desire to blaspheme His *Holy Word* or the *Holy Spirit*. We have previously discussed the breath of God, the breath of life, the wind of God, and emotionalism. Now let us look at the subject of speaking in or with other tongues.

It doesn't sound possible that an element such as the wind should be cohesive with tongues; nevertheless, the wind of God and the tongue of man are one of God's favorite areas of interest concerning the gospel, as the tongue can stir up a whirlwind of both good and evil.

"And there appeared unto them (as it were) *cloven tongues* (different dialects of languages) *like as of fire,* (within their spirit) *and it sat* (individually) *upon each of them"* (creating emotional praises) *"...and they were all filled with the Holy Ghost,* (of promise) *and* (each one) *began to speak with other tongues,* (languages/dialects) *as the Spirit gave them* (intelligible) *utterance"* (Acts 2:3, 4).

The sound of the Spirit coming upon them was likened unto *a mighty rushing wind*. (It was not the infilling of the *Holy Ghost* that brought forth the sound, but rather, the response thereof.) It was as though God was again breathing into man's nostrils, and while He was breathing, they all began to speak with (or in) other tongues or languages (Acts 2:3 & 4).

Now we come to the part of the puzzle that enables us to understand these connections of the Genesis scenario concerning the image of God, (Gen 1:26) and the breath of God, (Gen 2:7). However, before we can finalize this segment of thought, we must first become familiar with the expressions hereto written concerning "...*rightly dividing the Word of Truth*" (2 Tim 2:15).

Modern theologians have tried to explain away the *speaking in tongues* by saying it was only for that time and event, because it was the birth of the church. I debate their theorem, and challenge any and all to show forth one reason why God would suspend one part of the New Testament Covenant before its time. Not one "*Jot or Tittle*" of the Old Testament Law was rescinded until all was fulfilled. Which means: No part of the New Testament Covenant can be repealed until all is fulfilled.

We will finalize these connections by showing also how speaking with tongues qualifies believers to be the joining factor in the plan of salvation, and how (Acts 2:3,4) connects it all together from Genesis to Revelations–Let's get started.

Like most Pentecostals who attest their experiences of speaking in tongues, I responded in the same manner. But when it came to answering all those questions of why and how: Is it necessary, is it the initial evidence of the infilling of the *Holy Ghost*, and is there scriptures, which supports and/or sustains this claim? I must admit, that many times I have been at a loss for explanations and scripture quotations. But we were not concerned about that back when we were first baptized with the *Holy Ghost*, because we wanted only to tell the world about our new experience. However, not being a Christian or a student long enough to have learned the *Holy Scriptures*, our testimonies, many times, were an embarrassment to the truth.

Our mentors, though they tried, they needed more time to instruct us not to argue or debate scriptures. But being young and full of zeal, we would ride heavily upon the backs of people who were wandering in spiritual darkness; we tried to shove it down their throats. We jumped at any opportunity that dashed up before us. We grabbed at words and threw them at people hoping to make a homerun; but our swings were as bad as our aims, which brought us shame and embarrassment. What we didn't know about debating scripture was: It is never scripture against scripture, but always wits against wits and opinion against opinion, and we didn't know enough to have either or. O, the arguments we got into to no avail. O, the corners we were backed into and could not explain our way out without exposing our ignorance.

We had experienced the *"other tongues"* resting upon each of us and it was like fire shut-up within our bones. We went everywhere trying to *"spread it abroad"*–poor pastor, poor people, poor gospel, and poor God. I have often wondered how our pastor could tolerate our zeal that was *"...not according to knowledge"* (Rom 10:2). We spoke so much gibberish in trying to explain the plan of salvation that it is a wonder that even God could understand us. Not that we published an untruth, but that we could not explain it the way it was suppose to be explained. We listened to our teachers and mentors; we studied and we learned all we could. Yet, still, we loaded our slings with sharp stones, (sharp words) which wounded many that were searching for the truth. We were a dangerous band of crusaders that was more of a threat than a blessing to the cause.

There have been many times that God was not in my feet, my hands, my eyes, or my mouth, and it was because of my ignorance. *"God is not the author of confusion"* (1Cor 14:33) and anytime there is confusion, whether on the street or in church, there is always an evil work of some type hidden, even under the cloak of sincerity (James 3:15,16,17). What may appear as an angelic opportunity, ignorance will still give birth to some type of evil. If while preaching, teaching, or your witnessing causes confusion, (even while you're speaking in tongues) God is not the author of your feelings or your actions, regardless of how glorious your display. God does not send *mutterance* through His *Holy Gift*; His *Spirit* is genuine and each *utterance* by the *Holy Spirit* is a clear and direct conformation of its reality. Whenever the *Word of God* is being spoken there is no need of tongues or prophecy or edification; it has already been spoken through the ministry of the *Written Word* and needs no other trumpeteer.

I sat eleven-years under the teaching ministry of one of the greatest Bible teachers of his day, and remained in his fellowship until his passing in 1978. Not one time did I hear him speak in tongues during a church service: Not while he was teaching, preaching, praying, worshiping, or otherwise. There were times that we had, what we call a runaway service: where everyone started shouting and dancing and worshiping and speaking in tongues all at the same time. And I remember more than once the bishop came by me on his way out to his car, because he would not stay. He would take me by the arm and would say, "I hope these people can live for God when they come back to earth." His sentiments were: When you stop the preacher from preaching you stop the voice of God from ministering: for "...*faith cometh by hearing, and hearing by the word of God*" (Rom 10:17). He believed it was more important to have your emotions and your devotions adjusted to the *Word* so that the one would not overtake the other.

Though Paul said, "*I thank my God, I speak with tongues more than ye all*" (1 Cor 14:18). I do not recall reading one place within his writings where he spoke in tongues in church or in a public meeting, and neither do I find where any of the other apostles did so. To worship in the Spirit is to worship with the mind of the Spirit, and that, according to the *spoken Word*. If your worship is out of control, you are out of control, because the second half of that verse reads: "...*and in truth*" and *truth* is always in alignment with the *Spirit* (John 4:24). The expression "*They were all in one accord*" or "*Every one was in the spirit*" is a way of saying they were all of one mind. To be led by the Spirit simply means to be motivated by the *Word of God*. Because everyone is displaying the same emotions does not mean everyone is in the right spirit.

But is there a legitimate likeness between these twin-flames–the *Spirit* and *Truth*?

It was the beginning of a new area of worship and under a new administration of the Spirit. God is very particular how people worship Him, and He has set forth the pattern in His *Written Word*. Were they wild on the Day of Pentecost? That depends on what you call wild. They acted according to the Spirit's leading, and the Spirit does not bring confusion. This was a brand new experience for the apostles: A new way of worshipping God had suddenly filled the room, which was especially strange and unorthodox to the Jews who were listening from the street below.

I believe we Pentecostal's go beyond the spiritual boundaries in worshipping God today and create our own rules and level of emotional ecstasies: a lot of times it appears more as a display than what we really feel from the Spirit. There is a way to dance before the Lord, just as there is a way to shout before the Lord, and there is a time and place to speak in tongues; but they should never bring confusion to the service or to visitors. To worship in Spirit is to worship in the spirit of worship and in the spirit of truth–truthful devotion.

Victorious testimonies and healings have ignited emotions of dancing and shouting, which have ushered in a spirit of jubilation across audiences just as it does at bullfights, ball games, and other sports events; people get excited over what they hear and/or see. True worship is a response to truth. To *"worship God in Spirit and in truth"* is to worship God as a Spirit with genuine devotion; we must have our hearts, our minds, and our bodies in unity. We cannot worship God according to the dictates of our personal feelings; it must venerate from the *Word of God*.

If your display of tongues does not edify the church, (including strangers) you bring only confusion to the lost and doubt to the believers: *"If therefore the whole church be come together into one place, and all speak with tongues, and there come in* (those that are) *unlearned, or unbelievers, will they not say that ye are mad?"* (1 Cor 14:23). Sinners are not as dim-witted as we suppose. Remember, God gave them a mind to discern right from wrong just as He did with us. *"Tongues are for a sign..."* and not for a display; they are a symbol of expressions uttered by the *Spirit of God*. However, we Pentecostals use them more for a gesture of our spiritual greatness rather than a symbol of our humility. If people would speak in tongues more in their closets at home than in their church, I believe, more would be accomplish through their hidden repose than their public propose. If you want an open reward in church, God said, you will find it in your closet at home in prayer (Matt 6:6).

Nevertheless, as the news and noise of the strange speeches spread throughout the city of Jerusalem, the crowds then came together to hear of this new phenomenon. Our cities want to know the meaning behind our great services before they come to see; they have already heard the news, it's the real experience they're now looking for. Can they find it in your church service, or has the false display turned them away?

The apostles received the gift of the *Holy Ghost* while in the upper room. The noise of their style of worship caused an inquiry among the people downstairs, which was now spreading throughout the city. After this *Holy Ghost* experience was over upstairs and everyone had stopped speaking in tongues, then they all went down stairs where the service took on a different meaning. Upstairs it was jubilation–downstairs it was explanation. Now was time to explain the sound of the *"rushing mighty wind"* and the *speaking in other tongues*; it really does help if you can explain your emotion factors.

The overspill of their devotion and the strange sounds of their speech (*cloven tongues*) were recognizable by some on street below, which got the attention of the whole city. One thing for sure, their emotions might have been a little out of the ordinary while they were up-stairs, but when they came downstairs to explain it–they had it all together. When the Spirit first came into their lives and they began speaking with other tongues, they were, as it were, in a trance of devotion. (These *cloven tongues* were divided by nature because of the different nations represented. Some theologians believe that only the twelve apostles were speaking in *cloven tongues,* and they base their thoughts on the scripture: "...*are not all these that speak Galileans*" (Acts 2:7). Perhaps they should ask the Galileans.)

But on the other hand, this could hold a truth because of their history of expulsions and captivities. But then again, that would be denying that the others received the gift. Most of the foreigners spake the Aramaic dialect, whereas the natives of Israel (especially in Jerusalem) spake the Hebrew dialect. However, each of their dialects had a Semitic history, which originated through their expulsions from their homelands and captivities within other nations. Thus, the Aramaic dialect was more confusing, (corrupt–broken–mixed) whereas the Hebrew dialect was more pure (logical) to the crowd; nevertheless or whichever, it happened, and your guess is as good as mine.

If I know and understand Pentecostal people, they had a *Holy Ghost* explosion upstairs of dancing and shouting and staggering as though they were filled with new wine–explaining the mocking of (Acts 2:13). It took a while for the people downstairs to run to and fro throughout the city to spread the news of this strange type of devotion. It was not their mutterances that got the attention of the crowd, but their pure and distinct utterances–prompting an inquisition.

I must confess, some Pentecostals have really put on a show, and I really wonder what people think about those whom they know and see every day. They loved us as sinners even with our strange ways. But what do they think of us now as

Christian's worshipping in a strange way? Does our display of worship appear genuine in their eyes?

We Pentecostals should be so particular with our style of devotion as not to display ourselves as did the idol worshippers in the days of Elijah, (1 Kings 18) who tore down their altars and cut themselves as an expression of their devotion to their god; Elijah did not approve of it and neither did the Apostle Paul. There was a need for the apostles to speak fluently to the mixed multitudes of nations gathered at this *Feast of Pentecost:* It was their greatest anniversary service of the year and God used it as an opportunity of change for the nation.

Many Pentecostal services around the world have witnessed foreigners receiving the *Holy Ghost* by them speaking in a known dialect other than their own. Moreover, since there is a question as to what the apostles uttered, read it for yourself: *"Parthians, and Medes, and Elamites, and the dwellers in Mesopotamia, and in Judaea, and Cappadocia, in Pontus, and Asia, Phrygia, and Pamphylia, in Egypt, and in the parts of Libya about Cyrene, and strangers of Rome, Jews and proselytes, Cretes and Arabians"* (Acts 29-11). Every foreigner that we have preached to who received the *Baptism of the Holy Ghost,* all spake words of praise to the Lord and not that of prophesy. There was no need for tongues of prophecy on the Day of Pentecost, because the out-pouring of the *Holy Ghost* was the fulfillment of prophecy. The apostle Peter reiterated this from the words of the prophet (Joel 2:28).

It was the opinion of my mentor that when you receive this glorious gift, the type of tongues spoken depends on the type of people present. However, after you are filled with the Spirit, if you cannot or do not speak in tongues in your closet at home in prayer, you are wasting your time trying to convince others by your speaking in tongues in church. If the Spirit cannot overflow at home in the closet, it is strange how it can overflow in church; even the apostles question this type of display.

If you want to edify your soul, speak in tongues in your closet. If you want to edify your life, be a soul winner. If you want to edify the church, give forth a logical prophecy that needs to come to pass in your church. If you really want God to be proud of you, go knocking on doors, passing out tracks, visiting hospitals and nursing homes where humility lives in reality. But in church, the call is not for unknown *mutterance* but for intellectual intelligible *utterances* of the Word of God, lest you fall into condemnation and make a mockery of the Holy Ghost. "*Tongues are for a sign;*" they have their purpose and meaning. And if you are speaking in tongues without a purpose or meaning, the apostle Paul said, "*You are speaking into the air*"(1 Cor 14:9).

Sadly, however, some people seem to use their speaking in tongues to gauge as to whether or not the *Holy Spirit* is still in their life. They feel: that if they speak in tongues in church, whether by *utterance* or by *mutterance*, they still have the *Holy Spirit* within. This is a misconception; the *Holy Ghost* cannot be measured by this sequence. But you can measure it by your prayers, your repentance, your confessions, your desire to read the *Word of God*, and by witnessing.

Two factors remain in place that increases and/or decreases the power of the *Holy Ghost* within our lives: *Hearing* or *not hearing* the *Word of God*. Our emotions and our faith need a continual substance to survive: The more of the *Word of God* we receive, the more our faith increases. The *Word of God* is the venerator of true emotions: If we promote the *Word of God*, it will promote true worship, and the gifts of the Spirit will appear as witness.

Another remaining factor of truth concerning *tongues, utterance,* and *mutterance*: Many Pentecostal ministers really brawl-beat their subjects with rages of arrogance; this leaves their people and their service in spiritual derision. So, how can a person feel so elated to speak in tongues when they have just been beaten with pastoral cords of trepidation? And there appears yet another question: Along with tongues comes also a change of life. How can we speak in a heavenly language when we cannot speak the truth on earth? Regardless of the purity and sincerity of the sound of tongues, there must be a true change within to express a true change without.

Though tongue-talkers claim to be under the influence of the *Holy Spirit,* somehow the world can tell the difference between our *utterance* and our *mutterance.* Like water: When your life is full and overflowing with the Spirit, the water of life will be pure. But when you are low and near empty, the sediments of your life will be noticeably floating on the surface of your character and your spirit will leave a bad taste, even to a thirsty soul. (A.W. Pink, from his book "Exposition of Hebrews" explains it best, quoted from the works of John Owen 1616-1683[4]) "God never required the observance of any rites or duties of worship without a previous warrant from *His Word.* How thankful should we be for the *Written Word."*[4]

How can we tell the difference between *utterance* and *mutterance?* Simple: When it is done *"decently and in order",* (1 Cor 14:40). You cannot gage the indwelling of the *Holy Spirit* by your speaking in tongues. St. John has given us the best indication yet: *"By this shall all men know that ye are my disciples, if have ye love one to anther"* (John 13:35). Like Paul, He places love above speaking tongues (1 Cor 13:1). God is love, and when your love for souls is gone the Spirit of God is gone. Or, just ask your spouse, your children, or your neighbors; they monitor our lives every day.

King Saul is a great example of the Spirit leaving our lives without us knowing it. The most noticeable sign of its departure from our Christian lives is through their knowledge factors: We lose track of things that once we held of great value but is no longer necessary: King Saul lost his ability to discern the will of God and he became bitter and uncontrollable. This arrives by not building on a solid foundation but sinking sand. The sad part was: Saul did not realize his anointing had departed until it was too late. However, in the Old Testament the Spirit was resting upon them like a mantle–a cloak. But in the New Testament, the Spirit is within us and is renewable through repentance and by the renewing of our mind, (Rom 12:2) isn't that grand.

Chapter 18

Decently And In Order

This is another strange expression concerning the *Spirit of God*: Spirits are not something you can pour out as water. Nevertheless, when God filled these men and women (all one-hundred and twenty) with the *baptism of the Holy Ghost*, it was likened unto water being poured out upon them. *"And it shall come to pass afterward, that I will <u>pour out</u> my Spirit upon all flesh..."* (Joel 2:28). The people who heard this holy commotion from the *upper room* went throughout the city spreading the news, but it was not until nine o'clock in the morning that the crowd had fully gathered.

There have been many different versions of this Phenomena of Pentecost. One thing we do know is this: It was the *Day of Pentecost*, they received the *baptism* of the *Holy Ghost*, they spake with cloven tongues, they stopped speaking in tongues, they went downstairs, and it was at this point that the crowd had fully gathered, of which, representing about nineteen different nations (Acts 2:9-11).

(The native Jews, many years before, had migrated to other parts of the world and had learned other dialects, but with all probability they had either forgotten or were brought up never to learn their native tongue.)

The apostles and the others had stopped speaking in tongues, came down stairs, and began speaking in their native language–this would be practical. However, because of the large number of diversified visitors, there were also a large number of diversified languages; otherwise there would not have been a need for cloven tongues. And, for it to be phenomena, all in the upper room had to speak the same dialect.

Confusion in church is a pestilence that can only be eradicated through teaching; but sometimes a strong rebuke is an instant cure. I have seen people get up and walk out of church in the middle of a great service, not because God was not moving in our midst, but rather, because the worshippers were displaying emotions contrary to divine nobility. True devotions create true emotions acceptable by visitors and of God; otherwise, we offer up false advertisements. It would be wise in respect to the nature of the Spirit if holiness if people would all speak and act on the same level of passion and devotion; diversions of either are confusing to the world and could bring despite to the spirit of grace.

When Peter saw the multitude that had gathered to find out the meaning behind the commotion upstairs, it was not the time to continue speaking in tongues, but an opportunity to minister to the lost. If the church is full of righteous people, then let the church have another *Pentecost*. However, if there are sinners among the congregation, and most of the time there is, then it is time to minister the *Word of the Lord*. If we over-ride the ministry of the *Word of God*, we over-ride the will and voice of God, because *"faith cometh by hearing"* and if there is no preaching, faith will not come near; therefore, or for this reason, sinners will not repent. Are we then to do away with tongues in church? No. But rather, *"let all things be done decently and in order"* (1 Cor 14:40).

Chapter 19

Caught Up Into Paradise

There are many interpretations as to what exactly happened on the *"Day of Pentecost,"* and to tell you the truth, I wasn't there, as that was before my time. So I can only verify through what is written in the *Word of God*; namely, through Peter, Paul, and Luke's testimonies of the event. This was a national Holiday for the nation of Israel and many people had gathered to represent their brethren from different parts of the world, etc., which created a language barrier. But please note: Peter was addressing only the dwellers *"of Judaea, and all ye that dwell at Jerusalem,"* (Acts 2:14) because they were the ones who were hosting the feast, and they all understood what Peter was saying–keep this in mind.

I will not say that I can explain precisely the way it happened; however, with the help of a great church father (St. John Chrysostom 346-406) I will offer a small insight:[10]

"Number One: The phenomena had to happen on this day, the *"Feast of Pentecost."*

Number Two: It was essential that this event happen during this feast, and those who witnessed Christ's crucifixion would now also witness the token of its fulfillment.

Number Three: The mentioning of *new wine* is right opposite the *wheat harvest* and is not relevant to this day.

Number Four: *"A rushing mighty wind"* was always essential to this *"Feast of Harvest"* to separate the wheat from the chaff, which is here referred to in relation to the Spirit." (St. John

Chrysostom calls it more of a blast of wind rather than a mere rushing of wind.)[10]

When the *Holy Spirit* enters into an individual's life, it is supposed to separate the chaff from their lives and create a spirit of meekness within like unto the nature of a dove (Matt 3:16). However, somewhere or somehow, during the new birth of the Spirit, many people seem to receive a spirit far opposite from the nature of a dove, which results from bypassing the power of repentance. When the Holy Spirit is *poured* out upon a multitude, it is like the spreading of liquid fire, which creates a sound like a rushing mighty wind of praise, which blows the doubters away. (I have seen this with my own eyes and not through another: The sound of clapping hands and voices lifted high to give praise to God is like the sound of a rushing mighty wind.)

Since there were so many diversified languages present, there needed to be a phenomenal (out of the ordinary) experience witnessed because the apostles spoke only one main dialect. Nevertheless, being, as it were, *"cloven tongues"* (diversified tongues) came from one source and was distributed to many. They did not see fire, they did not feel wind, and they did not see the *Holy Spirit* descending like a dove. However, what they did sense in the Spirit was the likeness of the wind around them and the likeness of fire within them when the Spirit came into their lives.

Number Five: "God's actions are never foolish or without purpose: Whether in nature, in the elements, or in our lives, He is sovereign and always has a reason behind the season."[10]

Many years ago a great man of God within the apostolic faith wrote a book entitled "Why Did God Choose Tongues." It was an inspiring little book, especially for us who were young in the Lord; as we wanted to discover everything we could about God and our new experience of speaking in tongues. However, since I have grown in knowledge and in view of *"Anthropomorphic expressions,"* my studies have changed my

How Do Giants Fall?

opinion and my viewpoint has shifted somewhat to believe otherwise, as we shall discover further into this book. The book's theme pointed toward man's inability to tame the tongue–I certainly do agree with that part; however, I have found a greater enlightenment that I want to share.

First, I would like to point out to the reader, that when those who received the *baptism of the Holy Ghost* in the book of Acts, (Acts 2:4) or within any other New Testament setting: (Acts 8:15,16/10:46/19:6) they all spoke in or with other tongues; some known and some unknown. No one in these settings received this gift of the *Holy Spirit* without the original confirmation of speaking in or with tongues–this is an indisputable scriptural fact. The speaking in tongues at the birth of the Spirit are different from the indiscreet tongue-talkers mentioned in (1 Cor 12 & 13). And to those who say that tongues shall cease, they should re-evaluate their thoughts, because at the same time tongues shall cease, knowledge shall also cease, and not too many ministers or students will admit to their ignorance (1 Cor 13:8).

There was no way I could enter into this next phase without first creating a transitional bridge to help the reader(s) cross over from one concept of thought to another without becoming confused. Thus, the transition concept is on this wise:

There are tongues that are known and there are tongues that are unknown. When I received the *gift of the Holy Ghost* there were no foreigners present, so there was no need for me to speak in a foreign dialect. However, I did speak in Deity Dialect (unknown tongues) as the Spirit gave me the utterance, just as others experienced throughout the book of Acts. The style and operation of the Spirit was somewhat different but the experience was the same. Had there been a foreigner present, perhaps I would have spoken in their language as a witness. The time and place and surroundings determine the style and mode of the Spirit's operation of tongues. However, there is one thing you can, in every respect, depend upon: If it is the

Spirit speaking, it will be genuine *utterance*; otherwise, it will be nothing but *mutterance*, or, as the Apostle Paul called it: *"... speaking into the air"* (1 Cor 14:9).

The tongues (languages) the disciples were speaking in, though diversified, were understandable to some within the crowd downstairs (Acts 2:2-11). The speaking in the unknown tongues, (Deity Dialect) every believer should earnestly seek to experience this during private devotions (1 Cor 14:2). The order for speaking in tongues for all phases of this gift is set forth in (1 Cor Chapter 12). It was necessary for the *cloven tongues* to appear (not literally) on the *Day of Pentecost* because they were prophetic tongues (Joel 2:28). However, the unknown tongues mentioned in Paul's writings (1 Cor 14:2) are not prophetic by nature, but rather, by promise, and was and is for personal edification (Gal 3:14). And it was these unknown tongues that Paul heard while experiencing the caught up into the Paradise phenomena.

When the Apostle Paul was caught up into paradise, he heard a language he could not translate; he heard expressions that were beyond his ability to understand. So he spoke only of what he heard and said nothing of what he saw, because he saw nothing. People who say they have been to heaven are caught up into a fantasy and need to relax on the couch and let the kind doctor listen to their story. You cannot go into heaven being flesh and blood; you must be translated to enter into that holy place. And when or should you get there, you cannot leave, at least not until Jesus Christ returns to earth, and that will not be until after the great tribulation period. Once you get to heaven you are there to stay. No one within the entire Bible went to heaven and returned to earth to tell about it except our Lord Jesus Christ. Many may have had dreams and/or visions–but not in reality. Some did go there, that is true, but none have returned.

The Apostle Paul, though he spoke several languages, he could not decode what he heard while in this heavenly state of mind. Even the Apostle John, the diviner of visions and revelations, not even he could unravel the mysteries he heard and saw. But did you notice how that God did not reveal the secret codes of the language to St. John, nor to Paul; they both were left in the dark concerning heaven's secret language.

With all this said: Are we to abolish or abandon these figures of speeches and expressions concerning the Father, the Son, and the Holy Ghost, etc.? I would say not. Reason: It's part of the secret that has been hidden since the foundation of the world. But since the apostles and others used these terms within their writings, we must then continue in the same manner of speech, but also with the same attitude and zeal.

Chapter 20

The Witness Of The Spirit

We turn now to the scripture concerning where the Apostle Paul was caught up into, what is called, the third heaven, also called paradise, and then we will return to the *Day of Pentecost* and the speaking in tongues.

Imagine, if you will, this was a brilliant young man with all the same infirmities of the flesh as we, yet he was caught up into a place where they spoke an unknown tongue and he could not understand it (2 Cor 12:4). But was he caught up in the flesh, in the Spirit, was it a divine revelation, or was it an inspiration of the Spirit? (I can relate to this: When I received the revelation of *baptism in Jesus Name* and the *Oneness of God*, I thought I had been caught up into heaven–but it was a heavenly state of mind that I entered into.) The Apostle Paul could not explain his divine encounter, only that it felt like something beyond the limits of reality–a sensation that was out of this world.

But how is this scripture concerning Paul's visit to this heavenly state of mind "*...caught up into Paradise*" and hearing unlawful utterances; how is it connected to or in relevant to speaking in tongues on the *Day of Pentecost*? This scripture is the final connection, which proves that no one receives the *baptism* of *Holy Ghost* (*Holy Spirit*) without the initial conformation (evidence) of speaking in tongues.

Some say that they received the *Holy Spirit* by faith and not as it happened on the *Day of Pentecost*. Let me remind Bible students: You do *not* receive the Holy Ghost or the Holy Spirit by *faith*; you receive it only by *promise*, and that through obedience to the *Word of God*; as promised, when promised, and how promised (Joel 2:28). When the *Holy Ghost* was first poured out on the *Day of Pentecost,* it was a gift of promise that through Abraham all nations of the earth be blessed (Gen 22:18). The promise was recertified through the prophet (Joel 2:28) paid for on Calvary, sealed at the resurrection, and was delivered on the day of Pentecost.

Nevertheless, when the *Holy Ghost* was first poured out, the believers went wild with joy: They shouted, they danced, and they got loud, silly, and happy as the joy of the Lord filled their hearts. They worshipped God in a new and living way contrary to the traditions of their fathers. (I hear the gritting of teeth from the orthodox readers who think otherwise–but stay with me and think in terms of correlation of speech and not with human reasoning and you will see the truth.)

First, there is this question about the *third heaven,* also called *Paradise,* and the validity of the quote itself, as to whether it was an anointed statement or was it by the word of knowledge from these two poets: Aratus and Epimenides (Aratus: 315 BC–240 BC, and Epimenides, which Paul had read about, and, you have to consider his audience. You will not find any other place within scripture concerning there being more than one heaven, not in the Old Testament nor in the New Testament. No other apostle or prophet spake of there being more than one heaven. St. John the beloved was the only apostle privileged to view into heaven, and that only through an inspired vision and not in the flesh, and he made no mention of a second or third heaven–so we have no witnesses.

If there were more than one level in heaven, wouldn't that mean that there is also more than one level of Christians? Perhaps the average Christian would be placed on the first level, the more dedicated on the second level, and the perfect ones on the third level. But then there would have to be another level for the Throne-room where God sits, and that would make four levels. This subject is extensive and is worthy of study, for clarity, for understanding, for truth, and for doctrine to restrain the runoff of fables.

Was this a figure of speech concerning the *third heaven* and *paradise*, or was it an old pagan mythology that existed hundreds of years before Paul's day? The truth is: The Apostle Paul quotes the pagan poets Aratus and Epimenides (Aratus: 315 BC–240 BC, and Epimenides, who lived during the 6th century BC).[2] Paul was well aware of where most pagan quotes came from and he knew also the mind of his audience. It is this author's belief that there is a great mystery hidden behind this quote concerning the *third heaven* or *paradise*, more than there is the a realistic view. If there had been more than one heaven, the apostles would have told us so from their catalogue of divine visions and revelations; however, they did not, and you have to turn to history to find your answer–history compliments scripture.

All the fables that people come up with of them seeing spirits and visiting heaven: Of them going there and talking with Jesus and seeing God the Father and Mom and Dad; not even the apostles were granted these beholding's, and Paul heard only but saw nothing. When St. John saw into heaven through the eyes of the Spirit, there was war and rebellion going on between good and evil angels. And when he saw the Son of man, His eyes were as a flame of fire, he had feet like brass, and a sword came out of his mouth; (Rev 1:14-16) that does not sound like a place of tranquility to me.

There were also flying creatures with six wings and a great red dragon on the loose, having seven heads and ten horns, with a tail that could sweep the stars away (Rev 12:3,4). And you tell me that these people who were caught up into heaven didn't see these things–were they blind? What part of heaven did they visit? One final note: When and if you go to heaven, you do not return to earth until Jesus returns to earth to set up his government at the beginning of His Millennial reign. Not one prophet, not one priest, not one king, not one saint, or ruler in the Old or New Testament; not one went up to heaven and returned to tell about it–save our Lord Jesus Christ.

Many people have told of their experience of going there and returning to earth. This is a contradiction to the scriptures because "*...Flesh and blood cannot inherit the kingdom of God*" or the kingdom of heaven (1 Cor 15:50). Only the translated bodies of the saints will enter into that *Divine* abode, and once they are there–they are there to stay.

As I studied this subject, I found that there were many beliefs and opinions among the Jews as far back as the bondage in Egypt. (It appears this experience of fourteen-years past was revived in support of Paul's apostolic authority, and was directed toward those who challenged his apostleship (See 1 Cor 9:1-14, 2 Cor 10:8-15). His purpose within this statement was to establish his authority as an apostle without boasting of supernatural experiences. The reason of his reference concerning *Paradise* and/or the *third heaven*, was that the Corinthian people (church members and none-church members) still held to an old pagan tradition that the atmosphere just above our heads was the first heaven, the sun, moon, and stars was the second heaven, and beyond what man cannot see was the third heaven.

You have to consider the type of people that lived in the Corinthian province before you can form an opinion as to whether this statement is relevant to his experience or to their beliefs. Paul was no dummy and no man's fool. If he had explained it to them through any other channel of thought the people would not have received it. This statement, however, has convinced many generations of educated theologians to believe that there is more than one level of heaven–even apostolic ministers. This mythology began thousands of years ago when men began to study the stars, but has now been absorbed as a truth as well as a legend: It is part of the doctrine of Astrology–Stargazing–better know as Zodiac signs,

Horoscope, Palm readings, and practices of Ziggurat (human sacrifices as) offerings, which is Witchcraft. Paul was trying to create a relationship; a connection factor with these people and he attached it to his experience as an avenue through which he could minister to them. They well knew of the poets Paul was speaking about, so he used them as a connection factor to gain their confidence. It's not a sin to add seasoning to your message, even oil and wine, to help unify cultural differences.

However, in the case of being *caught up*: The verb *caught* (*ekstasis*) is not in the transporting tense–sense; it is a verb of enrapturing, of inspiration, entrancing, as in captivating, or being swept away in thought, and not that of conveyance of the flesh. It is the same verb as used in the case with Philip– being *caught* away in (Acts 8:39). Of John–being *carried* away in the Spirit (Rev 17:3, 21:19). Of Peter–falling into a trance (Acts 10:10). And also, concerning Paul falling into a trance when warned of coming danger (Acts 22:17). The verb is in the inspirational tense sense: speaking of visions and of revelations– but not that of being airlifted. W.E. Vine explains as thus: "A condition in which ordinary consciousness and the perception of natural circumstances were withheld, and the soul was susceptible only to the vision imparted by God."[9] God is not in the transportation business. However, He is in the inspiration business, and He can take you to heaven and back at the speed of thought in the Spirit and it can feel identical to reality. How did the devil show Jesus all the kingdoms of the world in a moment of time (Luke 4:5)? at the speed of thought. Thoughts can make you a king or a beggar in a moment of time. Man travels around the world and back at the speed of thought in the mind. Thoughts can make rich or poor, famous or unknown, all at the speed of thought. Our minds work faster than the speed of light (186,000 MPS). Salvation comes to us at the speed of thought: We travel from a world of sinful darkness into His world of marvelous light–all at the speed of thought.

(I like what a traveling minister once said: He was boxed in while traveling on a train across Europe, and to strike up a conversation he ask the man sitting across from him if he believed in heaven. The man quickly replied: "Yes, I was just there this morning–in prayer." At least he had his priorities lined up.)

After Paul had returned to earth (so to speak) from this heavenly experience, his reaction was somewhat questionable: "*...he was caught up into paradise, and heard <u>unspeakable words</u>, which it is <u>not lawful</u> for a man <u>to utter</u>*" (2 Cor 12:4). That sounds simple. But since when has it become unlawful to speak in any language–heavenly, earthly, known, unknown, or otherwise? While studying his statement closely, I took careful notice that the word *lawful*, as used in the Greek tense, which means: What Paul heard did not make sense. Thus it should read, "*It is not sensible for an earthling to utter.*" But why the statement: "*...not lawful to utter*? As strange as it sounds it does make sense.

Paul, after this experience, was writing to a church that was filled with Greek philosophers, orthodox Jews, and Gentile idol worshipers, which had intermarried and then had experienced the new birth. The mixture of their past created a divers representation of the *Spirit of God*. (We have this today in our churches). And like so many new converts of today, they too were eager to tell of their new experience. The problem was: They did not sit still long enough to be taught the rest of the story, so they did not understand the operation of the Spirit or the administration of speaking with tongues. There are many strange writings throughout the scriptures, and if pastoral leaders do not understand or search out their meaning, their people will remain in spiritual darkness, and confusion and fables will continue to thrive.

Paul said: He heard a language while in this ecstasy of mind that he did not understand, and that it would be unlawful or immature to try to mimic it. This is where the dividing line appears between *Utterance* and *Mutterance*. Though Paul spoke several languages, this one confused him.

In essence: This is about the same words that Peter used on the *Day of Pentecost* concerning their speaking in tongues upstairs, and none of it made sense to those downstairs. The manifestation of God's *Holy Spirit* was related to a *rushing mighty wind*; but it was that heavenly language that Paul said made no sense. The heavenly Spirit was flowing into the disciples untranslated–direct from Paradise. They could not help but speak in that heavenly dialect, because they were being filled with the Heavenly Spirit; Deity dialect is the only language they speak in heaven. And when that Heavenly Spirit came down to earth, naturally it sounded strange to those who heard it on the street. Why? It is the language of the Spirit world. So, then, when someone receives the *baptism of the Holy Ghost*, the heavenly Dialect is its witness. And that is why people speak in tongues when they receive the *baptism of the Holy Ghost*; the unknown tongue is the Spirits witness of the new birth (Rom 8:16)–mystery solved.

But the agnostic's say that they understood what the disciples were saying–and that is true. However, as I wrote in the previous chapter: The tongues on the *Day of Pentecost* were prophetic by promise: Promised through Abraham–Prophetic through the prophets, and received by promise on the *Day of Pentecost*. Remember, it was the unknown tongues that made no sense to the mockers. And still today, the gospel makes no sense to those who know not God. It is strange how that two people can hear the same message and one will understand and believe and the other will not.

Another witness to this great truth is found in (1 Cor 13:1) where Paul wrote, *"Though I speak with the tongues of men and of angels..."* He separates the two languages as one of earth (of men) and the other of heaven (of angles) otherwise he would have mentioned only one.

Just for the sake of the agnostics: The angelic hosts of heaven can speak any language or dialect they choose, as they are sent around the world to minister to the heirs of salvation. And just as Paul said, it didn't make sense, so also does the world say the same. It is amazing how every scripture is fitly joined together to validate the anatomy of truth (Eph 4:16).

Chapter 21

How Do Giants Fall

"And David put his hand in his bag, and took thence a stone, and slang it, and smote the Philistine in his forehead; and he fail upon his face to the earth" (1 Samuel 17:49).

One of the greatest strategies of overcoming your enemy is first, knowing their strength and weaknesses. Secondly, knowing your own strength and weaknesses. And thirdly, knowing your allies. If you know who your friends are and that they will stand with you, you will never have to worry about who is behind you, because your friends will always be there for you in body and in spirit. However, in this case of David facing Goliath, God seems to be his only ally.

In the day in which we live, most likely it will be you and you alone facing your giant, as God will, as with David, separate you from your flock of friends and family, and yes, even from church members that you trust and lean on so much. God, at times, will even separate you from your pastor, just to see if you can handle your situation alone. In David's case, he had the army, his brothers, and his king watching from afar. God had separated David for this occasion for him to gain fame among the warriors; it was just another step toward his calling as king of Israel, and Goliath was just another promotion factor along the way. How about you, dear friend; the type of obstacles you are facing today could be a promoting factor instead of just another day of hard times?

Friend, do not rest in the assurance that your friends and church members will run to your rescue when your giant blocks your way. Oh, yes, some may come out to watch from a far as you engage with the powers of uncertainties. But do not despair being alone. God does not send the whole church when He is interested in your capabilities; this is just another way of forcing you to discover your own fortitude. David's giant appeared as a rough hairy mean massive creature from a prehistoric age, but yours might appear as gentle and delicate as Bathsheba. Whichever, when your friends, church members, and your pastor all step back to watch the show, then you will know how David felt when he was climbing the ladder of success; but be careful, you don't want to miss a step and take a tumble as he and turn to politics as a way out.

It's not so much the size of our giants that frightens us, but the strangeness of the situations. David, killing Goliath seems to have been a breeze, according to the way the story reads. But later in life another giant appeared through the fashion of a beautiful woman. This time David did not fair so well; this time his giant attacked his nature. David well knew his own abilities in the art of physical warfare; but this time his enemy appeared in a different uniform with different techniques, which were strange to his war strategies. Self-confidence in spiritual warfare is not faith but a fools dream. It is best never to think to highly of yourself that you cannot be dethroned; you might be surprised at who you really are. Know yourself, and know your enemy before you engage into spiritual warfare, lest they chew you up and spit you out before all.

We will now take a look at this big fellow called *Goliath the Philistine*: The word *giant* is derived or translated from a root word which signifies to *fall* or to *fall upon*, and it conveys the idea of apostasy from true religion, signifying a violent invasion of others rights...as a persecutor and tyrant.[2]

This giant was the enemy of Israel and he was invading their territory, not only so, but was defying and challenging their trust and faith in God. But this is what spiritual warfare is all about when troubles come–maintaining trust and faith in God. Israel's record of overcoming their enemies was second to none–war was their favorite sport; but why the sudden change of heart?

Trouble can appear in many types and forms that can really confuse even the children of God. I have seen many strong Christians fall on their back in defeat, especially when their enemy appeared as an unknown factor. Not understanding the reason why has been a defeating factor for many spiritual warriors who put their trust in their physical strength instead of their shield of faith (Eph 6:16). Faith says stand still and see the glory of the Lord–the flesh will negotiate.

Our enemy is no more or no less than an evil spirit, and he is trying to defy the true church, which we as members should be aware of. David may have put to death the giant and removed his head, but Goliath's spirit is yet very much alive within the hearts of people today who are just as devilish in trying to frighten the people of God (1 Peter 5:8).

In reality, Goliath was not a Philistine by birth, as so many Bible students believe. Though the Bible states expressively *"Goliath the Philistine,"* still he was not a Philistine at all. In fact, there were no giants within the Philistine race–check your history. Though he lived among them, his genealogy goes back to the Rephaim's who in earlier times occupied the whole country of Palestine–that's how it got its name. Goliath's forefathers migrated into this strip of land many years before the Caphtorim's or Philistines invaded it and took control (Deut 2:21). His family remained in Gaza, and as the story goes, Goliath and his brothers became the champions of the nation in the days of King Saul and David (1 Sam 21 & 22). Goliath was of the Emims tribe…a people who migrated from the land of Ammon, and it was they that were a people of great statue

(Deut 2:10-11). Their migration might have begun around the time of the invasion by the Philistines (1250 BC). Nevertheless, some of the Emims tribe may have fled and migrated into the Gaza area, including Goliath's ancestors, as history states: They lived among the Philistines until the days of King Saul and David (about 1000 BC). Doubtfully however that Goliath was alive at the time of the migration but was born at a later date. Because of his great statue and strength, Goliath became a naturalized citizen among the Philistines and a national hero for their nation.[6]

By the given description of Goliath in (1 Samuel 17:5-6) this fellow must have been fit for the battle beyond any doubt or possibility of being defeated, especially by these little grasshopper people. The small Israelites could not have been a threat to this colossal enemy; but when he challenged their God he bit off more than he could chew. There could not have been any competition against Goliath's size or his appearance, as he stood upward above ten (10) feet, whereas the Hebrews stood only at an average height of five (5) feet tall–weight wise: 150 pounds against 1000 pounds plus.

Goliath, with eyes as large as a cow or horses eyes; to the Israelites he was a frightening creature to even look upon. With a mouth large enough to bite a small man's head off or crush his skull with his large teeth. With hands large enough to completely cover the face of an Israelite and smother him to death, or literally pull his head off his body. With feet so huge that with just one-step forward he could crush a man to death. His breathing must have sounded like that of a big black-angus bull, and to hear his roaring voice really terrified the little warrior's thoughts. Standing up or lying down, he would frighten anyone into a fearful loss of consciousness; he would have been an attraction for a circus if he could have been converted. History tells us that the giants were from nine-foot-three inches to ten-foot six inches, and some even over thirteen feet tall–your choice.[6]

This strange Leviathan came out every morning and every evening and roared like a mammoth lion. His voice was loud like that of a locomotive horn echoing across the valley floor, which created frightening imaginations within the hearts of these little warriors. Yet, and strangely, his cry was for just one man to come out and fight with him–just one. You would think that the king of Israel would have been the first to volunteer for the safety of his people; but King Saul was a smooth-handed and self-centered ruler.

(I see this as an overgrown bully in a neighborhood wanting someone to come out and play. Christians need to understand, that the most vile utterances from a sinner's mouth is the result of an inward torment within his or her heart, and they should be taken as a plea for help–they are under the influence of an evil spirit and their roaring (cursing) is no less than a cry for deliverance.)

David did not stroll into this situation by accident; it was predicated by the will of God to challenge David's credibility; after which the victory depended on his warrior skills. Christians, beware, there were other giants in the land in those days besides Goliath, and there are other giants in our day that appear just as colossal. There are many spirits in our world today that challenge us with the same purpose in mind: To defeat, to defy, to hinder, to destroy, and to thwart the will and purpose of God within our lives. Modern day giants are thoughts that are designed to challenge God within our lives, and if you have Jesus in your life, the anatomy of your thoughts will be pushed to the edge.

In my short time as a Christian I have heard many stories of those who were easily frightened because of their past. Not from a physical standpoint, but by ghostly images: From an old sin, an old habit or weakness they didn't repent, or, were too ashamed to confess. The night they repented and were baptized, their sins were washed away, but that opportunity will never return again through the same channel. It is not a sin to fear things of your past; old habits are hard to break, even after becoming a Christian. However, by not fully repenting of your past, your present could encounter many flashbacks, which could cause you to fear your future. Consequently, or because of this, it takes teaching from the *Word of God* to dispel these silhouettes from your new life of faith.

I remember very well the glorious day I was illuminated by the *Word of God*. My heart was opened, and at the same time *God* suddenly became real and alive in my soul. After repenting and being baptized in the precious *Name of Jesus Christ* and receiving the infilling of the *Holy Ghost*; I was so happy and excited that I was finally born again. At that point I thought I was a completely changed creature–until I returned to the physical world of reality to face again the seeds I had sown. I thought: I am free from my past; I'm a child of the King; so whys is my past still following me? I was so elated with this new experience that I thought I would never again be harassed by evil thoughts, etc., what was my problem?

I thought my old life of sin was forever gone from my life, and never again was I to face these vexations of the flesh–man was I wrong. My sins were placed under the blood–that is true, but my carnal nature did not change as planned. I found myself being buffeted daily by these common to human traits, and they kept me going back to the altar regularly to confess my weaknesses. The real formula for this problem was: When I was a sinner, all theses spirits had a key to my heart and they came and went as they pleased; I was not bothered by their presence because sin was a part of my daily diet–we all ate at the same table. But then Jesus Christ came into my heart; that was when the battle of expulsion began. My heart was like a large house with many rented rooms where these evil thoughts lodged, but when it came time to evict these rifts, my mind became a war zone of confusion.

Before, these spirits were not a problem; they satisfied my concept of life. But now that my concept has been changed, I no longer need their support; but evicting them from my mind has been a continual hindrance to my new life of faith. These spirits that once supported my carnal desires were now constantly and persistently trying to regain their habitation. What I had to realize was: I was still living in the same house (my fleshly body) and God had not yet made me into an angel with power–not yet. And after fifty-plus years of praying, fasting, studying the *Word of God*, attending Bible studies, seminars, and working in whatever capacity of Christian work I could find; I have yet to reach that angelic statehood–how about you? These unholy imps are still relentlessly pounding on the door of my heart–can you relate to this?

If the curtain of our lives were to be removed for the world to see our thoughts, we would all be shamed of the style of spirits we battle against. There is a long list of silhouettes from our past that constantly attack our new life style: Among the many is sex, tobacco, alcohol, fear, the lust of our eyes, the lust of our flesh, and, oh yes, the pride of life, etc., etc., of which these are the most common failure-factors. Christians should never be ashamed of the type of spirits they battle against; it is only human to war against the rhetoric from our past.

People, who were brought up in poverty, though they have overcome that stage of life, they still harbor fear of losing what they have. If they should drive through a city with ghettos and slums, each block they travel through serves as a frightening reminder of their past. One who was once a drunkard struggles with the memory of passing the local liquor store. Another, who was a slave to the tobacco habit, still fears its possessive power. Though their past has been forgiven and is under the blood; even after many years these spirits are still alive to them.

The giants of sex and lust are the two most to be revered. Where other spirits appear as ghosts of the past, sex is a part of the structure and makeup of man's nature, which blends into man's thoughts without upsetting man's behavior.

Pity the Christian who has rejected sound Bible teachings and Godly principles, because it is by these a man or a woman can discern the difference between lust and nature. These two have the same crave; however, nature knows not to go beyond the laws of righteousness, whereas lust will chance beyond its borders–we have many examples: Nature comes from within; lust comes from without. Nature is natural; lust is generic. Nature satisfies; lust pacifies. Sins of lust are forgivable, but sometimes forgiveness comes with shameful attachments that can wound a conscience and damage a reputation for life–Ask King David.

The Devil is always accusing Christians of their failures: Telling them that God has not forgiven them and that they are living their lives in vain. Mistakes happen when you miss a step scaling the ladder of life; failures happen when you look down and not upward. Every time you come to church or try to witness to a sinner the Devil will be there to remind you of your past, even naming and magnifying your faults in your conscience; telling you that the world and your church members know all about your failures and to testify is vain. When the devil starts reminding you of your past, remind him of his future.

Then there is the reality of your fall and the thoughts of what might be next. Then fear will attack your mind with thoughts of *"...a certain fearful looking for of judgment and fiery indignation..."* which will add to your already dejected spirit (Heb 10:27). Then the devil will try his final punch-line: "No use to pray, you failed, you sinned, you are no better than the rest of the world; give up trying, you'll never be a model Christian. If you go to church and worship the Lord you will be a hypocrite and your church members will think despicably of you; after all, they are the perfect ones and you don't fit in."

The devil is so good at lying, that most Christians, when they do make a mistake, they become cynical of God's forgiveness and believe the devil. This is a blind alley that is designed to strip Christians of their faith. It is amazing how Christians can discern the voice of Satan above the voice of God.

When the rock of faith struck Goliath between the eyes he fell forward on his face to the ground. I have heard some of these big three hundred pound football players fall to the ground while in competition for the crown, and man do they make a breath taking thud when they come down–Ku-thud–they fall to the ground. Wouldn't you just love to be the one they fall on, and then all those other three-hundred-ponders come jumping into the air and land on the top of the pile with you on the bottom? Not me!

Being a machinist for most of my working life I have worked with many types of people and machinery, and yes, I had some embarrassing moments–for example:

One day while running a lathe things were going just fine. I was setting on my stool and rocking forward to quickly re-adjust my in-feed dial (while standing on one foot) and then rocking back again to the comfort of my stool–I had it all timed. Everything was working perfect until I hung the heel of my shoe on my stool and pushed it out from under me, and down I went with a big thud–thump–thump–thump to the floor. The sound of the cabinet doors rattling, parts felling off the shelf and bouncing around on shop the floor; adding to the racketing sound of my clamoring fall. All the men working around the area saw and heard me as I went down. The humiliation and the laughs brought me more pain than did the burses–a lesson well learned.

It is strange how a fall can awaken us to reality and lead us back to safety; whether an evil or righteous desire, a sudden impact will alert our senses–physical and spiritual. A fall can change our directions, our attitudes, and help adjust our opinion of others. Sometimes a fall can be the best friend we have if we can get up with the right attitude. Is there a right or wrong way to fall and get up? Is there something symbolic or spiritual in the way we fall or get up? I guess it depends on

How Do Giants Fall?

the situation: In church it is a matter of prostration, out on the street it is a matter of embarrassment.

I heard a story of a man that said he was never down. His expression was: "I am either up or getting up." In other words: He counted his falls as an opportunity to get up again; and that is the hard part for a Christian–getting up again, and again, and again. Falling down and getting up is a natural part of a Christian's life while contending for the crown. You would think that one good flop after another would teach us how to stand up and stay up. Even though we display a clamor of mistakes and failures, it's only a part of the process of being up or getting up again and again and again–it's good for the knees.

There are some people who make a mighty good living at falling; that's all they do is fall. They fall from airplanes, cars, trains, motorcycles, bicycles, housetops, horses, etc., falling is their game and their fame; they are professionals in the field of falling. They have designed and developed their fall into a work of art. They are called a stuntmen or stunt-people, and they make millions of dollars doing nothing but falling and getting up again. However easy or hard or the pain they suffer they always get back up and try again–why not also a Christian? In my experiences as a clumsy person, regardless of how good or bad my fall, I cannot remember one time that it did not bring me some type of pain and/or embarrassment, as well as some well earned wisdom–know what I mean?

Somehow I catch a glimpse of Christianity today making an art of falling down. It is strange how that the fall of a giant some three thousand years ago is still an idiom to the church age. The holy scribes so meticulously recorded every move of these Old Testament eccentrics as an effort to warn, to instruct, and to inspire our contact with reality.

Even in the days of John, the Baptist` the real death fall of repentance had changed into an artifice of hypocrisy. But John was not the type of prophet or preacher to overlook such a valued virtue–he took it very seriously. Read an excerpt from one of his messages: *"And now also the ax is laid unto the root of the trees: therefore every tree, which bringeth not forth good fruit is hewn down, and cast into the fire."* (Matt 3:10). This was John's style of an altar call message that we just don't hear anymore.

The interpretation of this scripture is on this wise: By and through the power of the gospel, God is able to bring man down to the ground one way or another, and if it is the other, just the thought of being *"cast into the fire"* should bring man to his knees. We must not forget to prostrate ourselves before the Lord and not be careless about it. Bowing before a king in many countries yet today can mean life or death, depending on your pride or your humility of approach.

We have written a lot about David and how he brought down the giant; but did you know that even the way Goliath fell holds a symbolic excellence for the church of today? The laws of physics tell us that Goliath should have fallen on his back, but the laws of grace over-ruled the laws of physics and he fell on their face. The rock of ages in David's hands was like the gospel in the hands of a preacher; it will bring you to your knees. Did you know that if Goliath had fallen backward the whole story of David and Goliath would have proposed a different meaning? Falling backward is a sign of defiance and defeat; whereas, falling forward is a sign of prostration, humility and surrender. How we fall before the Lord in worship or in prayer determines the wave of the Sceptre in the King's hand. We may prostrate our bodies, but if our hearts are still standing we insult the spirit of grace. An evasive approach before the throne of God is as strange fire, which sooner or later will consume those who embrace an elusive attitude (Lev 10:1-3).

Less than a hundred years ago almost all denominations, after hearing the gospel literally ran and fell into the altar unto repentance. They didn't care who saw them or who heard them weeping over their sins. However, over time, religious fervor has dropped to a low-ebb through pride, and thus man has now perfected his fall until it is irrelevant. We hear the gospel and decide to get baptized without repentance: Repent of what? I'm a good person! What is there to repent of?

The ministry has lost its skill in striking people between the eyes with the gospel–the rock of ages. They have limited the gospel to only a small space of time; therefore, the power of the gospel cannot penetrate the shields of pride and doubt worn by those who trust in their cleverness. Whether in repentance or in prayer, man's approach into God's presence must be with his heart on its knees, his mind kneeling in humility, and his body bowing in prostration. By the stone striking Goliath between the eyes, he should have fallen on his back; however, by falling on his face he left us a display of how we should prostrate ourselves before the Lord.

Chapter 22

A Baptism Of Repentance

"John did baptize in the wilderness, and preach the baptism of repentance for the remission of sins" (Mark 1:4).

John, the Baptist` came on the scene at a time when there was much need for a change in the Law of the land, (which was the Law God gave to Moses). But since the nation had no separation of church and state, John's calling was to introduce a new bill (as we call it) of how sins would (in the future) be remitted. The old method of remitting sins had made no change within the hearts and lives of the people, so, thus, John, the Baptist` was chosen of God to be the liaison concerning this new manner of cleansing. *Water baptism* was something new and John was responsible for introducing it, espousing them to it, teaching it, and instructing on how it was to succeed the Old Testament Laws of purification.

To those who feel that John, the Baptist` ministry holds no significance for today, should return to their Bibles to refresh their memory concerning what Jesus said about him (Matt 11:11). I for one have wondered for many years why the scriptures read: *"For all the prophets and the Law prophesied until John"* (Matt 11:13). Why not until Jesus Christ? And also *"The Law and the prophets were until John"* (Luke 16:16). Again, why not until Jesus Christ? After all, it was He who was to replace the Law and the prophets. But why did their service end with John–or did it end with John?

When the children of Israel came out from under the Egyptian bondage, the night before their departure there was to be a lamb slain, and that Lamb was to them as the Savior is to us today–salvation and deliverance from the bondage of sin. However, there was something else that happened that night; it was to be the beginning of Israel's New Year. Their calendar as a nation was to begin on that night and not at the time of the giving of the Law. Before this time they existed just as any other nation: under the calendar of the world–from the time of creation. This is the natural Israel. The spiritual Israel, (of the church age) had its calendar change at the birth of Jesus Christ instead of at His death. With Israel, it was at the death of the lamb–with the church it was at the birth of the Lamb.

We will now study the significance of the time-frame between the Lamb slain, the departure from Egypt, the giving of the Law, the time-frame of the Savior coming into the world, of John's baptism, of the Saviors death, and the beginning of the church age at Pentecost? So, let's get started.

After Israel departed from Egypt then the Law was added to the nation as a Covenant–as a part of the pledge or promise God made to Abraham. There was three (3) months and fourteen days from the time of the exodus until the giving of the Law. But there was a Covenant already in existence at the time of the slaying of the Lamb in Egypt. How could they have been under the blood of the Covenant before the Covenant (the Law) was given? John, the Baptist' baptism: How could it have remitted sins before the Lamb (Jesus Christ) was slain? (Recommended studies: "Exposition of Hebrews by A.W. Pink. P513, Copyright 1st 1954, 18th 1994.)[4]

Number One, The children of Israel were at that time under the Abrahamic *Covenant of Promise* (not permanently secured by blood–only by random blood offerings). When they slew the Passover Lamb and left for the Promised Land, another part of the Abrahamic Promise was fulfilled: The blood of the lamb was shed the night before their departure, but was not yet added to the covenant until the Law was given. It would be another three months and fourteen days before the Mosaic Covenant would be given and the blood incorporated; whereupon, or until that time the blood of the Passover lamb had them covered (Ex 19).

Do you remember the words of Jesus when He was baptized of John in the Jordon River? *"Thus it becometh us to fulfill all righteousness"* (Matt 3:15). Another part of the Abrahamic promise was then fulfilled, but it would be another three and a half years before the Lamb of God would be slain.

Just as Israel was still under the Abrahamic Covenant of promise when the Passover Lamb was slain, so also was John's baptism under the Mosaic Covenant when Jesus was slain. When John preached *"A Baptism of Repentance,"* he was introducing the New Testament plan for the remission of sins—water baptism was to be henceforth for the remission of sin (Luke 3:3). However, John's plan of remission of sins was still under the jurisdiction of the Mosaic Law. John's baptism acted as a bridge to cross over from the Old to the New. Whatever the Law required for cleansing in the Old Testament still held dominion until the New Testament Lamb would be slain. *"... without shedding of blood is no remission"* (Heb 9:22). Thus, the remission power of John's baptism was good only until the New Covenant would come into effect, which, for the church, was not until the *Day of Pentecost*—but why not at Calvary?

Just as John's baptism looked back to the Paschal Lamb for its blood of remission, the church looks back to the Calvary Lamb for its blood of remission. And, just as the Abrahamic Promise reigned until the giving of the Law, so also did John's baptism reign until the *Day of Pentecost*.

Though Israel came out of Egypt on the first day of the month, it would be another three months and fourteen days (Ex 12:6) before they would receive the Law, which was then incorporated (in a type) into the Abrahamic Covenant of Promise (Ex 19). Everything pointed back to the promise God made to Abraham. In the Old Testament: There was the promise to Abraham, then the paschal lamb was slain, then the blood was applied, then the Law came and the blood was then incorporated into the Law. In the New Testament: Water baptism was introduced, then the Lamb of God was slain, and then water baptism was incorporated into the New Testament Covenant as a method to apply the blood for the remission of sin.

John preached a baptism of repentance for the remission of sin some three and a half years before the New Testament Lamb would literally be slain. John's introduction of *water baptism* was something new that he pulled from the shadows of the Law, and would be incorporated into the New Testament Covenant as a permanent method for sin's remission. But the new method would not begin its reign of sovereignty until the *Day of Pentecost*, fifty-days after the blood was shed, which also was another step in the fulfilling of the Covenant of Promise God made to Abraham.

The disciples mentioned in (Acts 19:1-6) who knew only the baptism of John; either they did not attend or perhaps left the *Feast of Pentecost* before Peter preached the full story. However, it did not take Paul long to make known unto them the rest of the story; after which, they were baptized in the *Name of the Lord Jesus*. Then Paul laid his hands upon them (V-6) and they received the *baptism of the Holy Ghost* and spake in tongues just as they did on the *Day of Pentecost*.

The gospel is designed to bring people to their knees in repentance, and this was the theme of John's message–repent! The gospel in his hands was as the stone of David; it brought people to their knees in repentance. John's message brought death to their old ways of thinking; it renewed their lives and gave them hope for the future. They laid their old lives down as dead men and accepted John's offer of a new life.

If we are to live like Christ we must then experience true repentance: Repentance is a death thing likened unto our Lord's death, water baptism is likened unto His burial, and receiving the *Holy Ghost* is likened unto His resurrection. We do not offer our bodies as a sacrifice for sin, but rather as a sacrificial death to sin, to arise and walk after His nature in newness of life. But for now let's continue our study of the ministry of John, the Baptist.

John's apparel might have been somewhat contentious, but his style and power of preaching provided the difference. From the obscurity of the wilderness he came walking into a world filled with spiritual and political corruption. His calling was to proclaim the message to the world that the Messiah had come, and John's voice and appearance drew the attention of just about everyone that saw him. His tongue was his sword, his speech was his shield, and the gazing flame in his eyes was his line of defense. Instead of running from him, (as from Goliath) people came out by the groves just for a closer look at this strange preacher from the desert. He did not have an array of fine linen to enhance his character (as so many of today who offer fancy arrays of refined speeches and clothing as a defiance against exposing their many imperfections).

John was his name and the baptizer was his title. What a name for a little giant; perhaps he should have been called *Little John*. He made his first appearance shortly before Jesus made His, and his cry for repentance would be heard throughout all the land of Palestine: *"Repent ye, for the kingdom of heaven is at hand"* (Matt 3:2). No promoter, no agent, no billboards, no announcements–just plain John, and he was just about as plain as he could get.

He was not a spiritual politician as many ministers of today; he had one purpose in mind: To open the door for the messiah to walk through and open it he did.

This is where so many preachers miss their calling: They do not want to be a doorman in the kingdom of God. Fame and fortune was no match for John's message or his appearance, he appeared, preached his message, and left without saying goodbye. His attitude was: *"He (Jesus) must increase, but I (the preacher) must decrease"* (John 3:30). Stardom and attitudes have always been a conflict of interest concerning the gospel and within the ranks of the ministry.

John came walking through the wilderness of Judea, and as he walked, he came to the place where he stepped out of the desert of obscurity (just as Moses) and onto the stage of action. When John opened his mouth to preach his first message, He cried with such a voice of decree that it brought thoughts to the mind of the people that this could be the first step toward freedom from political reign–but it was a different kind of freedom. His message ricocheted off the walls of a dispensational canyon that upset the balance of religious thoughts of those who ministered between the Old and the New Testament. The good news of salvation finally made its entrance into the world through this little giant, and he established a preface on the steps of Christianity that remains a memorial and legacy until this day.

What a preacher John was–Elijah has returned. Just out of the hot barren boring desert of loneliness, where he sheltered himself under a tent from the hot scorching heat of the sun. His nights were spent fighting the cold, the hungry jackals, deserts rats, and other creatures that scavenged through the night; including thieves and murderers on the prowl. Outdated, out of style, out of design, and out of fashion; he stepped out of obscurity right into the spotlight of evangelism, and with a voice filled with the power of Elijah, he pierced the hearts of the preferentials until they had a neurological breakdown. No special public training, no tent, no speakers or microphones, no soft seats, no music or singers; just a raw cut of flesh and bone. Yet he stripped sinners of their pride and brought them down in prostration with their faces to the ground–where has this type of preaching gone? The late Charles H. Spurgeon said: "If your preaching doesn't make sin stink you are not preaching."[7]

John really raised a national stink with his preaching. To some, John's voice was as the smell of sweet perfume, while to others his voice matched his body odor. Nevertheless, and regardless of his looks, his smell, and/or his costume of camel's hair: Without fronts, falsehoods, or any commemorative inscriptions of degrees to his name, he stepped upon the stage of time and became a champion of change. (Wouldn't it be wonderful today if our President, our Senators, and all our leaders would gather on the steps of our Nation's Capital and challenge all people to repent of their sins and turn back to God–I'm not holding my breath.)

With eyes bugged out and opinions raving, a man on fire with the gospel is what they saw from this scroungy smelly desert rat: *"...his raiment of Camels hair, and a leathern girdle about his loins; and his meat was locusts and wild honey"* (Matt 3: 4). (Try offering that attire and menu to your visiting evangelists and ministers across you fellowship–you will become famous over night.)

The gaze in John's eyes, the appearance of his clothing, and his brazen approach must have really gotten under the skin of the upper-crust theologians, as he challenged and exposed the nakedness of their methodic advantages. The nation of Israel was suffering from the same oppressions our world is suffering from today: Spiritual abuse and political corruption was on the rampage and John's messages exposed it!

John's appearance was liken unto the wild man who lived among the tombs from whom Jesus cast the devils out, and especially by coming fresh out of the desert. Think about this: His diet was as unusual as his looks. For a man of God he certainly did not carry the credentials of today's refined telecasters, nor would he meet the standards of today's dress codes.

As a young minister I was privileged to hear the late Bishop M.M. Hudson[8] as he preached about this desert rat called John. In his message: "A cousin to the King" he said: "John's hair was not combed, his clothing was dirty, he was smelly, his beard was not groomed, and as he ate particles from the locust along with the wild honey, dropped down and matted into his beard causing bees and flies and other insects to follow him in swarms everywhere he went. This became an annoyance to both him and to those who stood or sat nearby, and when he preached, he struggled against the flies and bees with one hand while gesturing with the other. He didn't carry the smell of today's arrayed and well groomed reverends, nor did he show the fine pleats of a hand-made suit; he was there on business– God's business."

His appetite was as strange as his looks. And another thing for sure, the ministry of today would not want to dine-out with him at their favorite restaurant after church on Sunday, AM or PM. And I doubt very seriously if he would make the overnight in-home invitation list or the elite offer to preach the National Convention, regardless of his name or fame; it would never be his dream come true. Yet, with all his unlikely attributes, John's message went out of his soul like a bolt of lightning and straight into the hearts of those who ventured out to hear him. His message was as the stone of David, which sank deep into their mind and down they went to their knees in repentance.

Not like the superficial altar calls of today at the end of a generic sermon, read by a generic preacher, taken from a generic Bible. John's sermons came straight from his heart, raw, uncut, unrefined, and it pricked the hearts of his audience, so much so, that whatever type of altar they could find, there they fell down upon it as dead men. When John cried, *"Repent ye, for the kingdom of heaven is at hand!"* His message punctured their orthodox hearts and pierced their heavy crust of self-righteousness that shielded their public image, and on into the core of their souls. The powerful force of his message brought prostration to their soul and spirit, and they fell face down to the ground in submission to the *Word of God*! They dropped down instantly, spiritually and critically wounded in their souls. Being condemned within their sinful hearts they surrendered their lives under the influence of the message John preached. He preached a baptism of repentance and his message brought people to repentance.

This is what happened when Philip the evangelist preached in the cities of Samaria: *"For unclean spirits, crying with loud voice, came out of many that were possessed with them…"* (Acts 8:5-8). What caused all the loud screaming, weeping, falling on the ground and crying out to God? It was the power of the gospel piercing their hearts until they fell on their knees and repented before man and God!

Most modern day ministers preach messages of hip-hop-ism to keep their audience in a dancing and screaming frenzy that is far from the school of John's day. This generation knows nothing about the real power behind the deathblow of the gospel of repentance. This is what the gospel is designed to do: To puncture the soul of man so all the corruption of sin can run out upon the altar.

If your repentance doesn't match the stench of your sin–you are wasting your time! If the gospel does not induce repentance from your heart–it is not the right gospel! Why do so many people pass through Pentecostal churches–why do they not stay? Answer: The old Bible teachers are passing on and this generation of preachers is not being taught how to *rightly divide the Word of truth*. The new generic gospel has no power to transform people into the image of God.

The Bible declares, *"All men mused in their hearts of John."* I have watched many people muse themselves on what the preacher was saying and/or what they saw during church service. However, within today's congregations, with its new mixtures of charismas and the new generation of generic believers, it can be amusing at times to the old heads of yesterday. The gospel is designed to be foolishness to the wise of this world. To fall into an altar and give up a sinful life is to the wise–foolishness! But to those who ponder, think, mull, and consider their sins and the possibility of them being lost for eternity, they drop their guard and throw away their shield of pride and reason and surrender to the power of the gospel.

They questioned what they heard from John: It went home with them, it ate with them, it walked with them, it talked with them, it went to bed with them, and they got up with it on their mind. The sound of Johns voice was like a trumpet continually warning them of their evil deeds and their need of repentance. He cried against the sins of their day: He cried against their religious leaders, against their hypocrisy, against the way they twisted the Law of God, and the way they ministered to the people.

Their sins were no different from our sins. Whatever type of sin it was, it was still sin and it was taking them to hell. John cried out against all their sins. He also challenged their deep-rooted orthodox traditions of worshipping God. John, like David, was not afraid to step out alone and face the giants of his day. Though not a colossal in statue and his dress code was not up to standard, yet he spake with the power and the spirit of Elijah when it came to standing up against the false prophets of his day (Matt 11:14).

One thing about the *Spirit of God*: John was small, but when the Spirit of the Lord came upon him to challenge unrighteousness his size was no concern. He was as significant as Elijah when he opened his mouth, and his message brought thought-provoking terror to his audience. His message terrified them into apprehension that they could be lost, and then it led them into repentance. The Bible is a book of *word pictures*, and John's message painted a terrifying picture of their future without God–the results of the factual gospel.

News of John's preaching had spread all around the country. He didn't have the refined voices of a large choir to help prepare the hearts of the people. He didn't have the songs we have today, nor all the beautiful musical instruments and talented singers to stimulate the mood of his crowd. He stood alone and he cried alone, *"Repent, for the kingdom of heaven is at hand!"* (Matt 11:14).

Just as the voice of John, the voice of the gospel is knocking on your heart's door today and asking you to repent. The secret and purpose of being submerged in repentance is to activate the power of the blood before being submerged in *water baptism*; without which, water baptism is useless in its power to set people free from their past.

Just as the blood was to be applied to the doorpost of the house the night the Lamb was slain; it was applied one time and one time only on that night. The blood was good for one application only–to stay the hand of death. So also is the power of water baptism: its purpose and power is good for one time and one time only. You have only one shot at the power of the *blood* in *water baptism*, after that–it is over. This is why *repentance* is so important–it activates the power of the blood in *water baptism*. Yet we have ministers today who baptize the same people so many times that the tadpoles have remembered their social security number.

The act of re-baptizing Christians in the same *name* is (according to St. Paul's writings) an act of witchcraft. How can it be an act of witchcraft and/or blasphemy? Witchcraft–in that it is deceptive. Blasphemy–in that it is a mockery of the blood of the Lamb. (Read Galatians chapter three.)

Witchcraft: Has to do with the rituals and repetitious acts of the ceremonial issues of the Law, which were repeated over and over each day, each week, each month, and each year. They could not make or keep the comers thereby perfect: *"For the law having a shadow of good things to come, and not the very image of the things, can never with those sacrifices which they offered year by year continually make the comers thereunto perfect"* (Heb 10:1). To lead a person to believe or to consent with one that their sins are being remitted again and again and again through this act of submersion in the *same Name* is an act of deception by the ministry, and thus, it is defined as witchcraft when they should have been restrained.

It was this part of the Law, the things which were against us: The repetitious daily, weekly, monthly, and yearly, acts of offering's and washing's and dipping's and cleansing's, over and over again that was done away with. The things that kept us bound repeatedly by repetitious rituals that were against us; Jesus, the Christ, nailed them (those ordinances) to His cross, (Col 2:14/Eph 2:14-17) and to command or allow without restraint those who have already been *baptized in the Name of Jesus Christ* is an act of witchcraft. To baptize them again and again would be placing them under the bondage of those same rituals of the Law; which, according to the Apostle Paul's writings, would be a double payment for the same debt of sin, and he tagged it as an act of witchcraft (Gal 3:1-29).

Blasphemy: Has to do with the sacredness of such a *holy ordinance,* which represents the power and the value of the blood that was shed for the remission of sins. The Bible teaches and we believe that the blood is applied in water baptism through faith in the *Name of Jesus*. To the ministers who practice the repetitious act of re-baptizing their people in the same Name–please read: Are we to believe that the Blood of Jesus is not able to *"Perfect forever them that are sanctified"* the first time they were baptized? (Heb 9:13, 14, & 10:11-14.) Are we to believe that through *water baptism* the blood is not able to wash away all our sins the first time–are there some sins that must be purged over and over again through the same logic?

Repentance is an earthly response to a divine call activated from heaven, and to baptize converts over and over again is to openly proclaim that the precious Blood of the New Covenant is not working as planned, and that the Blood of Jesus is no better than the blood of an animal (This is not my writings, my idea, my opinion, or my interpretation; it came from the Word of God, written by the Apostle Paul.) (Gal 3:1-13).

Baptism is a very serious and sacred ceremony and is not to be taken or entered into lightly. For the Blood of Jesus was far more sacred than the blood of an animal, and ministers who disrespect its sacredness will face a dreadful verdict, as the Apostle Paul wrote: *"He that despised Moses' law died without mercy under two or three witnesses: Of how much sorer punishment, suppose ye, shall he be thought worthy, who hath trodden under foot the Son of God, and hath counted the blood of the covenant, wherewith he was sanctified, an unholy thing, and hath done despite unto the Spirit of grace* (Heb 10:28-29). This is why the Apostle Paul wrote such an insurrection against the leaders of the Galatian church: They were trying to administer the New covenant of water baptism as under the manner of the Law, and that was the deceptive part, which Paul called *witchcraft*, and also perversion (Gal 1:6).

(This fact and factor applies also to the cup of communion: Pastors and ministers who serve anything less than pure wine for communion openly express their lack of discerning the Lord's body and/or the hallowedness of His Blood (1 Cor 11:29-30). Grape juice is not pure within itself until it has gone through the fermentation process: It must have a death to free itself from its impurities, and a resurrection of transformation before it can manifest its pure nature as wine; it represents the pure blood of the Lamb. Thus, by the same logic, they (the ministry) who serve anything less than pure wine for communion consider the Blood of Jesus to be no better than what they serve. Though wine is not as pure as the blood of the Lamb, yet Jesus chose it above all other resources, not as an example, but as *the only* example; cannot the ministry follow our Lord's example?

This makes me wonder: How do evangelists adjust their logic as they travel from church to church to face the next pastor's beliefs; how do they hold to their convictions without compromising the real truth–or do they have convictions?)

In the mid 1960's, an evangelist was telling our church about a great revival he had preached in northeast Missouri, where thirty people were baptized and filled with the *Holy Ghost*–I thought that was great. However, later that year I was near that church and decided to stop by for the morning service. It was a small church and their attendance record showed fifty last Sunday and fifty a year ago. The pastor was of middle age and in good fellowship with the organization. So, after service I questioned him concerning the fifty-a-year-ago, and the fifty last Sunday, and I also mentioned the evangelist, the revival, and the thirty who were baptized and filled with the *Holy Ghost*. He proudly said, "Yes! It was a great revival–we had a great time in the Lord." But when I questioned him concerning the attendance record and where are the thirty new members today, his countenance dropped to a low ebb.

The end of the story was on this wise: He told me that it was the same thirty that were baptized and received the *Holy Ghost* in the last revival, and the one before that, and the one before that, and so on. This pastor will face an austere inquisition before God for not restraining his people, and also for his attitude toward the precious *blood of the Lamb* and the *Holy Spirit*. The ideas that some church members conjure up through ignorance and self-will–it is amazing, yet pastors ignore it with pride. You will not find anywhere in scripture where any person was baptized the second time in the name of Jesus–it is not there. No apostle practiced it. So why do so many apostolic ministers practice something that is not scripture? It seems to be a fantasy of pride.

The Apostle Paul spent his life fighting spiritual ignorance, witchcraft, and perversion, yet the ministry continues to submit to such foolishness without fear of being held in contempt for not restraining their people. This type of ignorance can destabilize and undermine the fortress of truth until it becomes as neutral as any other modern religious body–but they don't have this problem.

Repentance can be repeated over and over again and again because it belongs to man. However, remission is a divine favor from heaven designed to purge man's sins by the blood through water baptism–here on earth. Jesus' death, burial, and resurrection, established the power of remission under the divine offering of Himself: He took the blood of that divine offering with Him into heaven, not just to sanctify man, but also to sanctify heaven itself (Heb 9:13, 14, & 10:11-14). My question is this: If the Blood of the Lamb can, with one offering, purify, sanctify, and cleans forever heaven itself, (from the pollution of the devil and the fallen angels) why is it that the same blood cannot sanctify one lost soul by the same principle?

In order to activate the power of the blood in *water baptism* the second time, our Lord would have to return to the whipping post, to the cross, to the grave, and thus, there must of necessity be also a second resurrection before there could be a second remission. Repentance is earthly and temporal, whereas remission is heavenly and eternal (Heb 9:26, 27). Once man's sins are remitted through water baptism, they are remitted. Remission establishes a burying place for sins repented thereof; after which, remission is achieved through repentance and confession. What remission does through water baptism, repentance and confession does after water baptism–it works like soap and water. If you sin after being baptized, repentance and confession is your only hope for cleansing. Being born again is repenting of your sins and being *baptized in the Name of Jesus Christ for the remission of sins*, and then you are a candidate for the gift (the promise) of the *Holy Ghost*; after which, if you sin, repentance and confession is your only avenue of renewal.

The expression of being born again and again and again of the *Holy Spirit* is another misconception induced by the same inventors of *multiple* baptisms. However, the truth still stands firm: There is only one *birth* of the *water* and one *birth* of the

Spirit. Everything the Law of Moses cleansed by repetitious acts, water baptism replaces; after which, repentance and confession is the only prodigal way. As for being refilled with the *Holy Ghost* or *Holy Spirit* over and over again: There is no refilling of the Holy Spirit on this journey.

Oh yes, there is a way to be born again and again and again, but it is on this wise: I was born in the flesh from my mother's womb. Then I was born again when I grew into my teen years and on into manhood. Then I was born again when I was baptized in *Jesus Name*. Then I was born again of the *Holy Spirit*. Then I was born again when I got married. Then I was born again when we had children–three times. Then I was born again when my wife passed away and then again when I remarried. Being born again is like entering into a new revelation of life, and believe me, I have had many revelations on life. There are many avenues, which lead to new births; but only once can man be born of the water and of the Spirit–handle with care.

There are many churches where you can find food for your soul, and there are many churches where your soul can be revived and renewed; however, there are no refillings of the *Holy Spirit*. Thus it becomes, not a matter of a refilling of the Spirit, but rather, a renewing of the mind (Rom 12:2, Titus 3:5). The Spirit of God dwells within our hearts, but it is through our mind that the Spirit does it work of faith, and that's where the big problem lies. There is a continual struggle between these two elements (the heart and mind) that wear down the one or the other until one says, "I give up" or the other says, "I am to faint to continue." It's not so much a power struggle but a communication factor, which means: The heart can overload the mind and cause it to faint, (Heb 12:3) and then the heart has no means through which to reach the outside world. "*Faith cometh by hearing*," but it is first analyzed within the mind where it is rejected or accepted before being released to the heart, and that is where man's greatest problems exist. God's greatest problem is getting past the mind to the heart.

The heart and mind work like computers work: The heart is the hard-drive and the mind is the monitor, which displays what the heart is thinking. Sometimes the heart causes the mind to crash by reason of an overload, and then the lights go out. Solution: Reboot. This gives the computer time to reset its defaults and re-adjust its processing procedures. Sometimes we humans need to reboot (repent) so we can reset our defaults, attitudes, opinions, and our priorities. The heart cannot go back to work until the mind is renewed. So, go ahead and reboot (repent) right now–your heart is waiting on your mind.

Repentance and confession revives, restores, and renews the spirit, the heart, and the mind. The scripture concerning: *"And they were all filled with the Holy Ghost"* (Acts 4:31). These were believers who were already filled with the *Holy Ghost* and needed no refilling. It is an expression of how the glory of God's Spirit descended upon them when they prayed and worshipped; the Spirit moved like fire caught in the wind and these believers were enjoying the warm breeze of the spoken *Word*.

Yes, the Gentiles received the *Holy Ghost* before they were baptized (Acts 10:44-48). However, it is a known fact and truth that repentance must be a prerequisite before salvation can be turned on. Repentance sometimes comes easy. But most of the time it's hard to find; especially for us Gentiles who know nothing about God or repentance. It depends upon the wisdom of the speaker and the power of the gospel, which they preach and/or the condition of the hearts of the people. These people that heard Peter preach that day or evening, whichever, must have previously repented in order for the *Holy Ghost* to fall (descend) upon them.

Some of the most complicated inventions have lain dormant for years before our eyes unnoticed and useless until someone said, "Lets read the instructions." Kings have caused cities to

How Do Giants Fall?

be saved from the wrath of God because the leaders of that city said, "Let's try repentance." They tried many things, but among the many there was just one thing that worked and worked right; there was just one thing that turned the wrath of God away from them and that one thing was repentance–repentance activates God's mercies.

John, the Baptist` was not sandwiched in between two dispensations, but rather, his message was an introduction and preface concerning the new administrator of the New Covenant. Thus, he became the earthly custodian of the heavenly transition, which joined the two together. Repentance is the bonding factor that every minister should take into account. John's design of submersion (water baptism) was conceived from the ideal of the *brazen Laver* in the tabernacle, where the priests washed before entering into the *Holy Place* to minister. It was a cleansing place where all who ministered were made clean. But John saw it as a pool for cleansing where the entire body could be immersed through the same principle. This is why both water and blood came forth from Jesus side–water and blood represent repentance and baptism.

Why do Christians struggle with their past after they come into the church? They did not fully repent of their past sins. Repentance is the first secret code of three, which unlocks the door of salvation, water baptism in *Jesus Name* and being filled with the *Holy Spirit* are the other two codes (Acts 2:38). There is only one true formula for salvation and it is the only one. It started on the *Day of Pentecost* and it will run until the end of this dispensation. Three easy steps: "*...Repent, be baptized in the Name of Jesus Christ, receive the gift of the Holy Ghost* (Acts 2:38). It was executed at Calvary, sealed in the grave, consecrated at the resurrection, and instituted on the *Day of Pentecost*.

If Jesus had not died there would have been no burial; without which, there would have been no resurrection; without which, there would be no eternal life. If repentance is of no value, why then did God set aside an entire dispensation for it? But why have so many leaders set aside something so pronounced as something so insignificant? Is it the new style and the new generation of generic believers? Did we not hand this truth down to them in the same package it came in? Have we failed to fulfill the Lord's command to preach the whole gospel to the whole world–including our children?

The gospel is the strand that connects us to Faith. Faith is the strand that connects us to repentance. Repentance is the strand that connects us to water baptism, Water baptism is the strand that connects us to the blood. And the blood is the strand that connects us to the promise of the Spirit. It is all connected together as links in the trivia of God's plan. Repentance is more than an expression of remorse; it goes far beyond that. Repentance expresses our intellectual approach to God. Our repentance must be as appalling as our sins, because it speaks of our willingness to surrender to God's will, expresses our recognition of our sinful state of mind, the shamefulness of our guilt, and it sets us out in the open as naked before Him–ever feel that way–naked on the stage of life?

According to W.E. Vine, Expository Dictionary of New Testament Words: [9] "Repentance helps us to express its meaning in perhaps a more intellectual or accurate way. As a verb: It helps us to perceive the implying change of the mind (Luke 24:45). As an adjective: It speaks of God in regard to his gifts and callings (Rom 11:29). As a noun: Repentance is an after thought of regret...to amend or resolve one's life as a result of contrition for one's sins"[9] (Acts 2:37). What then is remission? How does it work? Where can one find it in the Bible? How will it help us today?

John, the Baptist` came preaching the *Baptism of Repentance* for the *remission* of sin. But since the blood of the New Testament Lamb had not been shed, John's baptism was still under the jurisdiction of the Law. John preached to the people that they should bring forth fruits (behaviors) worthy of repentance before he baptized them (Matt 3:7-8). He would not baptize them until or unless they fully repented. (The word *unto* means: *in response to,* such as: in response to your message I repent and submit to baptism.) John's preaching was so powerful that it incarcerated the hearts of the people and brought them to their knees in repentance; accepting water baptism was their response.

What has happened to those days when the preaching of the gospel cut people to the heart? Have we by-passed a vital organ that leads to the blood-flow of eternal life? Have our spiritual arteries become clogged with errors and over-sights that we cannot discern its value or its necessity?

John saw the people as they were falling down and repenting; their tears of remorse convinced him to baptize them. He saw also those who had not repented; who showed no shame or remorse, and he refused to baptize them–that's the way it should be. What has happened to the old time stance of refusing to baptize where there is no repentance? Ministers today want to get people into the water as soon as possible as though they are afraid they would get off the hook. There is nothing fishy about it; if their repentance is genuine there is no worry about losing them.

The question is asked: In what name did John baptize his converts? He simply used the term: "*...that they should believe on him, which should come after him, that is, on Christ Jesus* (Acts 19:4). It was a temporary baptism designed to last only until the New Testament Lamb was slain, the blood was shed, and the plan was set into motion. That's why John's disciples had to be baptized again in the right name (Acts 19 1-6). Though the Blood of the Lamb was shed at Calvary, water baptism in the *name of Jesus Christ* was not incorporated into the plan of salvation until the Day of Pentecost; after which, the New Covenant was signed, sealed, and delivered.

Chapter 23

A Baptism Of Remission – Part One

We now know what repentance is, but what then is *remission* and how and when is it applied during the formula or application of our being born again–what part does it serve?

Remission simply means, to forgive or to terminate a debt, as in: "I have suspended your penalty."[7] The story of the prodigal son is the most common scenario: "*Remission* of the punishment due to sinful conduct."[7] However, the verb is always based upon the vicarious and propitiatory sacrifice in connection with the atoning factor for trespassing God's Law. Meaning thus: It is never our righteousness verses the righteousness of another; it is always our sin verses God's righteousness. Repentance is a type of death as though we had died; thus, in order for the *remission* of sins to be activated, the sacrifice of repentance must first be applied. If from the heart man does not appallingly and truly repent, his physical prostration, whether standing, kneeling, or lying on the floor–is meaningless.

A story of some fifty-years ago comes to my mind, of a young man who was asked to bring in some firewood for his mother. Like most young people who think they know more than their parents, he refused, and when his father approached him, the contention grew so defiant that the lad left home in a rage of anger. However, it didn't take long for the young man to learn a lesson in respect, especially after the cares of life fell upon his shoulders. On his return, just like the prodigal son, his father met him outside, and after a brief greeting, the lad asked for forgiveness and then asked if he could come inside. His father said to him, "Yes, my son, you may come inside–after you bring in the firewood." True repentance will lead you to true obedience.

If you think you can get passed the keeper of the gate without *repentance*–you are wrong. The lad's obedience was proof of his *repentance*, which brought *remission* and forgiveness. Repentance is the scale by which the keeper of the gate measures all who come to Him; once repentance is established, *remission* is then applied through obedience, and the *Holy Ghost* is the reward thereof.

The *Baptism of Repentance* is somewhat different from the *Baptism of Remission*. John, the Baptist' forewarned his audience to show forth a spirit like unto a *Baptism of Repentance*, because it prepares man for the *Baptism of Remission*, which prepares man for the *Baptism of the Holy Spirit*. John wanted to see his converts submerged in repentance before they were submerged in water baptism for *remission* of sin.

Yes, according to the writings of Mark and Luke: John preached a *Baptism* of *Repentance* for the *remission* of sin, but it did not hold the same significance as Peter's baptism in (Acts 2:38). There arises another question: If John's baptism was *for* "...*the remission of sin*", how could it offer *remission* since the blood of Jesus (the Lamb) had not been shed? It takes blood for sins to be remitted and the blood of the New Covenant Lamb had not yet been offered (Heb 9:22). But how could John's baptism offer *remission* without the shedding of blood?

When Jesus was on the cross, a spear pierced His side and there came forth both "*blood and water*" (John 19:34). Water does not offer any *remission* for sin; however, it does offer a powerful cleansing: Under the Law, the priest were required to wash their hands and feet in the *bronze Laver* before continuing their approach to the Altar where the atonement would be made (Ex 30:19). Water and blood, atonement and remission, and soap and water, all work for the same purpose–to cleans. The water sanctifies while the blood purifies, and remission is what you feel after both are applied. John, the Baptist` conceived his ideal of water baptism from the linguistic concept of the *Laver* (Ex 30:19).

The scripture in (Luke 16:16) *"The law and the prophets were until John..."* simply means: What the Law and the prophets said was still in force until that time. The reader must remember: John was the last of the Old Testament prophets and the first of the New Testament prophets, and Christ was the end of the Old Testament Law, (Rom 10:4) which means: The Law then rests` its case. The Law did not end the day John and/or Jesus were born–but the day Jesus died. Whatever types of *remissions* were offered under the Law was still subject to the limitations and approval of the Law, which also was to be renewed at the end of every ceremonial or atonement year. The *remission* attached to John's baptism, according to the Law, expired at the end of the sacrificial year.

The question arises concerning the disciples of John in (Acts 19:1-5) and the validity of their baptism: There was a sewing, a planting, and a harvest time. John was the sewer, Jesus was the Seed, and Pentecost was the harvest. John, the Baptist` baptism was temporal, just as the Paschal lamb under the Law was temporal: But the new method of *remission* would not expire because it was eternal. Because of the fifty-days between the planting and the harvest (Jesus` death and the harvest–Pentecost) John's method of *remission* remained sovereign until the end of the fifty-days; after which, the *Name of Jesus* was attached to certify its eternal power. It followed the type and shadow of the Paschal lamb and the law being attached at a later date. Plus, too, this is why the disciples of John had to be baptized again in the *Name of Jesus*–to certify their baptism.

As I have previously stated: All sacrificial atonements expired at the end of the sacrificial year. However, the blood of the Lamb did not certify John's baptism because the Law of Moses held sovereignty over all purifications. John's baptismal power of *remission* reign only from the day it was introduced until the *Day of Pentecost*, when a baptism certified by pure blood would be instituted and certified (given a name). And this is why we baptize in Jesus Name because the name certified the baptism. In the Old Testament *remission* of sin was certified through a daily, weekly, monthly, and yearly sacrificial offering made by the blood of an animal: each animal was offered according to the type of transgression of the individual. However, the yearly atonement covered all sins for the entire nation–but only for that year. John's new type of *remission* required also a new type of blood, which offered a new and better type of *remission*. Just as the blood of the Paschal Lamb held sovereignty until the Law, even so, John's baptism held sovereignty until the Day of Pentecost.

John's new Decree was sandwiched in between some timeframes that was shadowed from the past: The blood atonement for the newly formed nation was made the night before the children of Israel would depart from Egypt; but the law was not given until three-months and fourteen days latter. John's new style of sanctification (*water baptism*) began about the same time Jesus began His earthly ministry and remained in effect until the *Day of Pentecost*.

(We find no continuation of John's ministry after his death; however, the disciples continued John's method of purification until the crucifixion–it appears that no one was baptized between the Crucifixion and the Day of Pentecost.)

Just as Moses was forty days receiving the Old Testament Covenant, Christ was forty days instructing the disciples concerning the New Testament Covenant. The time limit on John's baptism was set to expire the moment the new atonement was made, just as was all other sacrifices, but because of the emblematic time period, it was left in place. When Jesus was baptized the Law of righteousness was fulfilled; there was nothing else the Law could say. When Jesus arose from the grave, having accomplished the redemption plan, *water baptism* received its eternal power by means of the blood of Jesus, but was not instituted until the *Day of Pentecost*.

The Apostle Paul, finding these disciples of John (some fifty years later) put him in a delicate situation where he must use wisdom. He seized the moment by carefully introducing them to the new era of sanctification: He offered the same method of cleansing but under, or into, a new *name*. And *"When they heard this, they were baptized in the name of the Lord Jesus."* How about you friend, have you received the revelation of water *baptism* in the *Name of Jesus Christ*?

There are some portions of the Law that is still in affect; however, under a different administration and under a new administrator–*Jesus Christ*. Our laws do not end or change because we elect a new president; (although some should) we simply elect a new administrator. Paul said, *"Christ is the end of the Law,"* the end of an administration (Rom 10:4). The Law's administration did not end at the beginning of the life of Christ but at the ending of His life; the moment He died the sovereignty of the Law (The temporal power of its *remission*) expired. John, the Baptist' was sent in to be the liaison of the transition from the Old Testament to the New Testament. He introduced a new bill or method for remitting sins and the new administrator of the New Covenant–Moses term as administrator of the Law was expiring and John was sent in to introduce the new administrator.

Another thing the reader must remember is: The Law still held jurisdiction over any sins remitted, personally and/or nationally, and therefore, the sins that were remitted under John's transition were temporary: No remittance or *remission* of sin was good beyond the year's end (Lev 16:34). Any type of justification before the death, burial, and resurrection of Jesus Christ was still under the jurisdiction of the Law. When Jesus Christ arose from the grave; He not only brought us out of sin, but also *"Blotted out the handwriting of ordinances that was against us…nailing it* (them) *to his cross,* (Col 2:14). He took away the *temporal power* of the Law's *remission* and incorporated it into the Law of grace–giving it *eternal power*. His Cross-made the things that were against us void; however, all other ordinances that were for us are still in affect, but now are certified by pure blood by a new administrator who understands its authority.

But why and how is repentance connected to this new method of *remission*? St. John Chrysostom offers to us some very important elements (with some omissions). [10] Quote:

"Then cometh Jesus from Galilee to Jordan," etc. "With the servants and with the criminals, the Lord, the Judge, cometh to be baptized. But be not thou troubled, for in these humiliations His exaltation doth most shine forth. For He who vouchsafed to be born so long ago in a Virgin's womb, and to come forth thence with our nature, and to be smitten with rods, and crucified, and to suffer all the rest which He suffered; why marvel if He also was baptized with the rest to His servants. For the amazement lay in that one thing, that being God, He would be made Man. For this cause, John also by way of anticipation said all that he had said before, that he *"was not worthy to unloose the latchet of His shoe;"* and all the rest, as for instance, that He is Judge, and rewards every man according to his desert, and that He will bestow His Spirit abundantly on all; in order that when thou should see Him coming to the baptism, might not suspect anything mean. Therefore he forbids Him, even when He was come, saying, *"I have need to be baptized of Thee, and comest Thou to me."* For, because the baptism was *"of repentance,"* and led men to accuse themselves for their offenses, lest any one should suppose that He too *"cometh to Jordan"* in this sort of mind, John sets it right beforehand, by calling Him both Lamb, and Redeemer from all the sin that is in the world.

Since He that was able to take away the sins of the whole race of men, much more was He Himself without sin. For this cause then he said not, *"Behold, He that is without sin,"* but what was much more, *"He that beareth the sin of the world,"* in order that together with this truth thou might receive that other with all assurance, and having received it might perceive, that in the conduct of some further economy He cometh to the baptism. Wherefore also he said to Him when He came, *"I have need to be baptized of Thee, and comest Thou to me?"* And he said not, *"And art Thou baptized of me?"* nay, for this he feared to say: but what? *"And comest Thou to me?"* What then doth Christ? What He did afterwards with respect to Peter, this did He then also. For so he too would have forbidden Him to wash his feet, but when he had heard, *"What I do thou knowest not now, but thou shalt know hereafter,"* and *"thou hast no part with me,"* he speedily withdrew from his determination, and went over to the contrary.

And this man again in like manner, when he had heard, *"Suffer it to be so now, for thus it becometh* (benefits) *us to fulfill all righteousness,"* straightway obeyed. For they were not unduly contentious; but they manifested both love and obedience, and made it their study to be ruled by their Lord in all things. And mark how He urges him on that very ground which chiefly caused him to look doubtfully on what was taking place; in that He did not say, *"thus it is just,"* but *"thus it becometh."* For, inasmuch as the point unworthy of Him was in his mind chiefly this, His being baptized by His servant, He stated this rather than anything else, which is directly opposed to that impression: as though He had said, *"Is it not as unbecoming that thou avoidest and forbiddest this? Nay, for this self-same cause I bid thee suffer it, that it is becoming, and that in the highest degree."* And He did not merely say, *"suffer"* but He added, *"now."* "For it will not be so forever," saith He, *"but thou shalt see me such as thou desirest; for the present, however, endure this."*

Next He shows also how this *"becometh"* Him. How then doth it so? *"In that we fulfill the whole law,"* and to express this He said, *"all righteousness."* For righteousness is the fulfilling of the commandments. "Since then we have performed all the rest of the commandments," saith He, "and this alone remains, it also must be added: because I am come to do away the curse that is appointed for the transgression of the law. I must therefore first fulfill it all, and having delivered you from its condemnation, in this way bring it to an end. It becometh me therefore to fulfill the whole law, by the same rule that it becometh me to do away the curse that is written against you in the law: this being the very purpose of my assuming flesh, and coming hither." *"Then he suffereth Him. And Jesus, when He was baptized, went up straightway out of the water; and, lo, the heavens were opened unto Him, and he saw the Spirit of God descending like a dove, and lighting upon Him."*

For inasmuch as many supposed that John was greater than He, because John had been brought up all his time in the wilderness, and was (the) son of a chief priest, and was clothed with such raiment, and was calling all men unto his baptism, and had been born of a barren woman; while Jesus, first of all, was of a damsel of ordinary rank (for the virgin birth was not yet manifest to all); and besides, He had been brought up in an house, and held converse with all men, and wore this common raiment; they suspected Him to be less than John, knowing as yet nothing of those secret things; and it fell out moreover that He was baptized of John, which thing added support to this surmise, even if none of those mentioned before had existed; for it would come into their mind that this man was one of the many (for were He not one of the many, He would not have come with the many to the baptism), but that John was greater than He and far more admirable: in order therefore that this opinion might not prevail with the multitude, the very heavens are opened, when He is baptized, and the Spirit comes down, and a voice with the Spirit, proclaiming the dignity of the Only Begotten.

For since the voice that said, *"This is my beloved Son,"* would seem to the multitude rather to belong to John, for it added not, *"This that is baptized,"* but simply *"This"* and every hearer would conceive it to be said concerning the baptizer, rather than the baptized, partly on account of the Baptist's own dignity, partly for all that hath been mentioned; the Spirit came in form of (or likened unto) a dove, drawing...the voice towards Jesus, and making it evident to all, that this was not spoken of John that baptized, but of Jesus who was baptized...See, for instance, what astonishing things are done, preludes of those which were to come; for it is no more paradise, but Heaven that is opened. But let our argument with the Jews stand over unto some other time; for the present, God working with us, we would direct our discourse to what is immediately before us.

"And Jesus, when He was baptized, went up straightway out of the water; and lo! The heavens were opened unto Him" (Matt 3:16).

Wherefore were the heavens opened? To inform thee that at thy baptism also this is done, God calling thee to thy country on high, and persuading thee to have nothing to do with earth. And if thou see not, yet never doubt it. For so evermore at the beginnings of all wonderful and spiritual transactions, sensible visions appear, and such-like signs, for the sake of them that are somewhat dull in disposition, and who have need of outward sight, and who cannot at all conceive an incorporeal nature, but are excited only by the things that are seen: that so, though afterward no such thing occurred, what hath been declared by them once for all at the first may be received by thy faith. For in the case of the apostles too, there was a *"sound of a mighty wind,"* and visions of fiery tongues appeared, but not for the apostles' sake, but because of the Jews who were then present. Nevertheless, even though no sensible signs take place, we receive the things that have been once manifested by them. Since the dove itself at that time therefore appeared, that as in place of a finger, it might point out to them that were present, and to John, the Son of God. Not however merely on this account, but to teach thee also, that upon thee no less at thy baptism the Spirit comes.

But since then we have no need of sensible vision, faith sufficing instead of all. For signs are *"Not for them that believe, but for them that believe not."* But why in the fashion of a dove? Gentle is that creature, and pure. Forasmuch then as the Spirit too is *"a Spirit of meekness,"* He therefore appears in this sort. Besides this, He is reminding us of an ancient history. For so, when once a common shipwreck had overtaken the whole world, and our race was in danger of perishing, this creature appeared, and indicated the deliverance from the tempest, and bearing an olive branch, published the good tidings of the common calm of the whole world; all which was a type of the things to come. For in fact the condition of men was then much worse, and they deserved a much sorer punishment. To prevent thy despairing, therefore, He reminds thee of that history. Because then also when things were desperate, there was a sort of deliverance and reformation; then by punishment, but now, on the contrary, by grace and an unspeakable gift. Therefore the dove also appears, not bearing an olive branch, but pointing out to us our Deliverer and suggesting the gracious hopes. For not from out of an ark doth she lead one man only, but the whole world she leads up into heaven at her appearing, and instead of a branch of peace from an olive, she conveys the adoption to all the world's offspring in common.

Reflect now on the greatness of the gift, and do not account His dignity the less for His appearing in such a likeness. For I actually hear some saying, that "such as is the difference between a man and a dove, so great is that between Christ and the Spirit: since the one appeared in our nature, the other in the likeness of a dove." What must we say then to these things? That the Son of God did indeed take upon Him the nature of man, but the Spirit took not on Him the nature of a dove. Therefore the evangelist also said not, *"in the nature of a dove,"* but *"in the form of a dove."* Accordingly, never after did He so much as appeared in this fashion, but at that moment only. And if on this account thou affirms His dignity to be less, the cherubim too will be made out by this reasoning much His superior, even as much so as an eagle is to a dove: because they too were figured into that visible shape. And the angels too superior again, for they no less have many times appeared in the fashion of men.

On this very account the Jewish baptism ceases, and ours takes it's beginning. And what was done with regard to the Passover, the same ensues in the baptism also. For as in that case too, He, acting with a view to both, brought the one to an end, but to the other He gave a beginning: so here, having fulfilled the Jewish baptism, He at the same time opens also the doors of that of the Church; as on one table then, so in one river now, He had both sketched out the shadow, and now adds the truth. For this baptism alone hath the grace of the Spirit, but that of John was destitute of this gift." St. John Chrysostom. [10] Unquote.

Chapter 24

A Baptism Of Remission – Part Two

Portions of this chapter are accessible from the writings of St. John Chrysostom, one of the most quoted of church fathers whose writings are now in Public Domain.[10] (Italics added)

I lingered at length in the last two chapters to lay a foundation for this chapter. Let us now attend to the sequel of what has been before said: Quote:

"When Nicodemus fell into error and wrested the words of Christ to the earthly birth, and said that it was not possible for an old man to be born again, observe how Christ answered more clearly to reveal the manner of the birth, which even thus had difficulty for the carnal enquirer, yet still was able to raise the hearer from his low opinion of it. What saith He? *"Verily I say unto thee, Except a man be born of water and of the Spirit, he cannot enter into the Kingdom of God"* (John 3:5). What He declares is this: "Thou sayest that it is impossible, I say that it is so absolutely possible as to be necessary, and that it is not even possible otherwise to be saved. For necessary things, God hath made exceedingly easy also. The earthly birth, which is according to the flesh, is of the dust, and therefore heaven is walled (with invisible barriers) against it, for what hath earth in common with heaven? But that other, which is of the Spirit, easily unfolds to us the arches above. Hear, ye as many as are un-illuminated, shudder, groan; fearful is the threat, fearful the sentence. It is not (possible) He saith, for one not born of water and the Spirit, to enter into the Kingdom of heaven; because he wears the raiment of death, of cursing, of perdition, he hath not yet received his Lord's token, he is a stranger and an alien, he hath not the royal watchword. *"Except,"* He saith, *"a man must be born of water and of the Spirit, he cannot enter into the Kingdom of heaven."*

Yet, even thus, Nicodemus did not understand. Nothing is worse than to commit spiritual things to argument; this it was that would not suffer him to suppose anything sublime and great. This is why we are called faithful, that having left the weakness of human reasoning's below, we may ascend to the height of faith, and commit most of our blessings to her teaching; and if Nicodemus had done this, he would not have thought it impossible. What then doth Christ? To lead him away from his groveling imagination, and to show that He speaks not of the earthly birth, He saith, *"Except a man be born of water and of the Spirit he cannot enter into the Kingdom of heaven."* This He spoke, willing to draw him to the faith by the terror of the threat, and to persuade him not to deem the thing impossible, and taking pains to move him from his imagination as to the carnal birth. Saith He, another birth, O Nicodemus. Why draw thou down the saying to earth? Why subject thou the matter to the necessity of nature? This birth is too high for such pangs as these; it hath nothing in common with you; it is indeed called birth, but in name only has it aught in common, but in reality, it is different. Remove thyself from that which is common and familiar; a different kind of childbirth bring I into the world; in another manner will I have men to be generated: I have come to bring a new manner of Creation."

(Here again our Lord is using *"Anthropomorphic expressions"* by transcending His speech from Deity Dialect to human dialect, using things common to man. But like so many people of today, Nicodemus failed to understand even though it was spoken in a language or expression familiar to him.)

"I formed (man) of earth and water; but that which was formed was unprofitable, the vessel was wrenched awry (amiss); I will no more form them of earth and water, but *"of water"* and *"of the Spirit."* And if any one asks, "How of water?" I also will ask, How of earth? How was the clay separated into different parts? How was the material uniform, (it was earth only) and the things made from it, various and of every kind? Whence are the bones, and sinews, and arteries, and veins?

Whence the membranes, and vessels of the organs, the cartilages, the tissues, the liver, spleen, and heart? Whence the skin, and blood, and mucus, and bile? Whence so great powers, whence such varied colors? These belong not to earth or clay. How does the earth, when it receives the seeds, cause them to shoot, while the flesh receiving them wastes them? How does the earth nourish what is put into it, while the flesh is nourished by these things, and does not nourish them? The earth, for instance, receives water and makes it wine; the flesh often receives wine, and changes it into water.

Whence then is it clear that these things are formed of earth, when the nature of the earth is, according to what has been said, contrary to that of the body? I cannot discover by reasoning, I accept it by faith only. If then things which take place daily, and which we handle, require faith, much more do those, which are more mysterious and more spiritual than these. For as the earth, which is soulless and motionless, was empowered by the will of God, and such wonders were worked in it; much more when the Spirit is present with the water to do all those things so strange and transcending, they easily take place?"

(This story before us is not of man's natural creation, but that of man's spiritual creation: Just as the dust possesses all the necessary compositions for the creation of Adam's body; even so the *Written Word* possess all the necessary compositions for the spiritual man. The *Word* spoken in creation is the same *Word* spoken through the gospel; it is the creative power on earth, which God has chosen to be His hands in forming the new spiritual man into His Image and likeness.)

"Do not then disbelieve these things, because thou seest them not; thou dost not see thy soul, yet thou believest that thou hast a soul, and that it is something different besides the body. But Christ led him not in by this example, but by another; the instance of the soul, though it is incorporeal, He did not adduce for that reason, because His hearer's disposition was as yet too dull.

He sets before him another, which has no connection with the density of solid bodies, yet does not reach so high as to the incorporeal natures; that is, the movement of wind. He begins at first with water, which is lighter than earth, but denser than air. And as in the beginning earth was the subject material, but the whole was of Him who molded it; so also now water is the subject material, and the whole is of the grace of the Spirit: then, *"man became a living soul,"* (Gen. 2:7) now he becomes *"a quickening Spirit"* (1 Cor 15:45). But great is the difference between the two: The soul affords not life to any other than him in whom it is; the Spirit not only lives, but affords life to others also. Thus, for instance: The apostles even raised the dead. Then, man was formed last, when the creation had been accomplished; now, on the contrary, the new man is formed before the new creation; he is born first, and then the world is fashioned anew (1 Cor 15:45). And as in the beginning, He formed him entire, so He creates him entire now.

Then He said, *"Let us make for him a help"* (Gen 2:18) but here He said nothing of the kind. What other help shall he need, who has received the gift of the Spirit? What further need of assistance has he, who belongs to the *Body of Christ*? Then He made man in the image of God, now He hath united him with God Himself; then He bade him rule over the fishes and beasts, now He hath exalted our first-fruits above the heavens; then He gave him a garden for his abode, now He hath opened heaven to us; then man was formed on the sixth day, when the world was almost finished; but now on the first, at the very beginning, at the time when light was made before. From all, which it is plain, that the things accomplished belonged to another and a better life, and to a condition having no end.

The first creation then, that of Adam, was from earth; the next, that of the woman, from his rib; the next, that of Abel, from seed; yet we cannot arrive at the comprehension of any one of these, nor prove the circumstances by argument, though they are of a most earthly nature; how then shall we be able to give account of the unseen generation by baptism, which is far more exalted than these, or to require arguments for that strange and marvelous birth? Since even "but if it is impossible to reply to these questions, how shall it not be more impossible to speak concerning the unseen and far higher generation? Or rather, how is it not superfluous to demand reasons," etc.

Angels stand by while that generation takes place, but they could not tell the manner of that marvelous working, they stand by only, not performing anything, but beholding what takes place. Let us then believe the declaration of God that is more trust worthier than actual seeing. The sight often is in error, *it is impossible that God's Word should fail;* let us then believe it; that which called the things that were not into existence may well be trusted when it speaks of their nature. What then says it? That what is affected is a generation. If any ask, *"How,"* stop his mouth with the declaration of God, which is the strongest plain proof. If any enquire, "Why is water included?" let us also in return ask, "Wherefore was earth employed at the beginning in the creation of man?" for that it was possible for God to make man without earth, is quite plain to every one. Be not then over-curious. That the need of water is absolute and indispensable, you may learn in this way. On one occasion, when the Spirit had flown down before the water was applied, the apostle did not stay at this point, but, as though the water were necessary and not superfluous, observe what he says; *"Can any man forbid water, that these should not be baptized, which have received the Holy Ghost as well as we?"* (Acts 10:47).

What then is the use of the water? This too I will tell you hereafter, when I reveal to you the hidden mystery. There are also other points of mystical teaching connected with the matter, but for the present I will mention to you one out of many...In baptism are fulfilled the pledges of our covenant with God; burial and death, resurrection and life; and these take place all at once. For when we immerse our heads in the water, the old man is buried as in a tomb below...then as we raise them again, the new man rises in its stead. As it is easy for us to dip and to lift our heads again, so it is easy for God to bury the old man, and to show forth the new. To show that what we say is no conjecture, hear Paul saying, *"We are buried with Him by baptism into death"*: and again, *"Our old man is crucified with Him:"* and again, *"We have been planted together in the likeness of His death"* (Rom. 6:4, 5, 6). And not only is baptism called a *"Cross"* but the *"Cross"* is called *"Baptism."* *"With the Baptism,"* saith Christ, *"that I am baptized withal shall ye be baptized"* (Mark 10:39) and, *"I have a Baptism to be baptized with"* (Luke 12:50) (which ye know not); for as we easily dip and lift our heads again, so He also easily died and rose again when He willed or rather much more easily, though He tarried the three days for the dispensation of a certain mystery" Unquote.

Chapter 25

A Baptism Of The Spirit

The Baptism of the *Holy Ghost* or *Holy Spirit* is one of the most controversial subjects within theological studies there is. It's not so much whether there is a *Holy Ghost*, but as to how or when one receives it: Do we receive it or do we not receive it? Do we, or do we not speak with tongues when we receive it? It's not so much as to whether we do or not receive it, but rather, the way we receive it that theologians disagree upon. Most all religious bodies will admit to the fact that the *Holy Spirit* was given on the *Day of Pentecost*, but they debate the fact that *speaking in tongues* is the initial evidence of its presence when man receives it.

Some say it comes by faith, but that is only a partial truth. It also comes through faith, which carries some guiding principles with it: To simply say "I accept the *Holy Spirit*" or "I accept the Lord as my personal Savior by faith" is a candid way of getting around the truth, and besides, this statement is not found within the *Holy Scriptures*. The expression "personal Savior" simply means: Salvation is now on a personal level and not national. It is a phrase used by the Protestant faith as a way of convincing their followers into believing they have automatically received it. You do not automatically receive the *Holy Spirit*, and you do not accept Christ as your personal Savior until you accept and obey the *Written Word*. Then, upon believing and obeying the *Written Word*, through repentance and water baptism in the *Name of Jesus Christ*, then Christ accepts you by filling you with the *Holy Ghost*; the infilling of His Spirit is your sign of His acceptance, and the speaking in tongues is the evidence thereof. If to say: "I accept Christ as my personal Savior" was the true way of receiving the *Holy Spirit*, Peter would have told us so on the *Day of Pentecost*–however, he did not and neither did any of the others. And besides, the Spirit came before they could say anything.

Some hide behind the scripture found in (Rom 10:9) which reads: *"That if thou shalt confess with thy mouth the Lord Jesus, and shalt believe in thine heart that God hath raised him from the dead, thou shalt be saved."* But there is a glitch hidden behind this scripture that few will admit to, and it is on this wise: This scripture was written to Christians who had already received the gift of the *Holy Ghost*: *"To all that be in Rome, beloved of God, called to be saints…"* (Rom 1:7). And also: *"All the saints salute you, chiefly they that are of Caesars household"* (Philippians 4:22).

Many theologians tell us, that after the *Day of Pentecost* tongues ceased, because it happened as an act of introducing the *Holy Spirit* to the Jews and there is no further need of its evidence–but that is not true. They were still speaking in tongues throughout the entire period of the Acts (actions–activities) of the Apostles, (Acts 10:44-48/19:1-6) a timeframe that covered over a hundred-years. However, if tongues have ceased, it is because believers have ceased communicating with God through tongues. Yet, it has never ceased within the *Holy Scriptures*, because yet today people are receiving the same *Holy Ghost* just as they did on the *Day of Pentecost*.

One-thing Bible students should realize is this: The book of Acts is the only book in the New Testament that was written to sinners, for sinners, and about sinners. The four-gospels were written as an Introduction or Preface of the story and life of Jesus Christ; they are books of His lineage and biography; each from a different viewpoint. And from the first chapter of Romans to the end of the book of Jude, all was written to Christians, pastors and churches. The book of Acts is the only door through which man must enter to be saved, and Acts 2:38 is the only key that will unlock that door–try it and see.

Chapter 26

Lend Me Your Life

The misconception of God is so widely spread that even the elect of the Spirit filled people are being deceived. We write about God in the way we think: We relate to Him from our frail human viewpoints because we are down here and He is up there, and thus, our finite minds produce thoughts and words uncharacteristic of His existence. However, *God is a Spirit*, and in the spirit world things do not exist as they do here on earth. The reader may or may not consent, concur or agree with the following statements; nonetheless, for the sake of the point in view, the reader should consider the facts: The laws of Physics says, where there is no one to hear–there is no sound, or, where there is no man–there is no God. God exists, that is true–but how He exists is the question.

There are many viewpoints on this subject, but we are not writing about Physic's–but how God exists. Viewpoints matter within earthly creations, but not with God–the facts must come from the *Holy Scriptures*: *"For precepts must be upon precepts...line be upon line...here a little and there a little"* (Isa 28:10) to prove scriptural factors. We have physical (earthly) factors and we have spiritual (heavenly) factors. The physical relates to man's earthly creation, whereas, the latter relates to man's spiritual creation. Having said thus, we enter into this last lecture concerning the *Spirit of God* and *what is a spirit*–let us began.

How Do Giants Fall?

The first Adam was the seed of man; there was no female contribution, because all the necessary factors were within the seed. Since therefore (by the same reason and example) the second man, Adam (Jesus Christ) was the seed of the new spiritual man, which was created without male or female contributions. As concerning the sperm, blood, and Chromosomes, etc., seeds contain their own producing and reproducing factors; the womb was used as a surrogate incubator for its birthing process. There is not much difference between the womb and the grave; both offer a place of incubation unto new life, (Rev 1:5) keep this in mind.

There is this question: Not all seeds need outside germination; some can germinate by light, warmth, and moisture. Whichever or whatever, there remains an unanswered question: Many preach that Mary contributed the flesh for the body of Jesus, which has its contentions. But could it be that Mary's only contribution was the *microbiological* of her body for the surety of Jesus' birth? We cannot set this in stone, but it is worthy of thought due to the uncommon circumstances–let this stir your thoughts.

Man is an Anthropus–a human being. When God created Adam's body He placed within it everything He Himself wanted to be. The arms, legs, feet, head, eyes, ears, voice, etc., are all complimentary entities' added to compliment man's skills, motions, and communication factors. However, spirits have none of these features, and this is where the misunderstanding lies. Man is known as a human being (a humanoid) because he has a body, but God has none of these factors.

Let's look at it from a spirit standpoint: Whither it is Spirit, as in Deity, or spirit, as in created spirits, such as angels, none experience emotions like as man. Spirits can be neither happy or sad, laugh nor cry, angry or frustrated. All these symptoms and factors belong to man and man alone; they are all a part of man's temperament, which God placed within him at creation. Keep in mind: that when God created man, it was all a fantasy of what God wanted to be. But man could not comprehend the bases of his own creation so he went astray; but God did not go astray when He made man. Everything that God put into man was a part of what He wanted to be. Man was created to express all these feelings, including the power and wisdom of God. But since God does not experience emotion factors, He created man with a qualified temperament to fulfill or express these emotions. He wanted man to express what He Himself could not–but His plan crashed through man's ignorance of himself.

Let's climb out on a limb where we can get a better view. Before man God was nothing–He did not exist in reality. You cannot be something if you are nothing–there must be a point of expression and/or contact to be someone or some thing. So, in the beginning God created the heavens and the earth, not for Himself, but for man–but this did not satisfy God's frenzy to exist. Then, God created a man and placed within him a portion of His own Essence, which should have inflamed man to express God; but not even with divine qualities within did man show an interest in God.

(A lot of Spirit-filled people today are just as Adam when it comes to being interested in the nature of God. We find this within the attributes, wisdom, and knowledge factors of man; when God created man He was hoping to create Himself.)

The first man (Adam) was a prototype of God's dreams for the future of what He wanted to be. This is what Paul was writing about when he wrote: "*...the second man is the Lord from heaven*" (1 Cor 15:47). The first prototype failed, so God created a second prototype made of flesh and not of dust. Man was first formed by the *spoken word* and then brought to life. A Christian is first brought to life and is then formed by the *Written Word*– right in reverse.

When people look for God, they look for a body with a face, hands, and feet, etc., they look for the same qualities as man–but God is not a man. *God is a Spirit* and spirits do not have the same qualities as man. Nonetheless, when God was made flesh, He made Himself as close to man's characteristics as man is to himself.

The original plan for God to be man was through Adam; he was to express all the attributes of God: The power, the glory, and the wisdom of God–the masculine side of God. Eve was brought on the scene to express God's compassion and affection–the tender side of God. Let me say this again: Adam was to express the nature and/or the characteristics of God, whereas Eve was to express the nature and/or the characteristics of the church–only the married will understand this statement. Their bonding together as one was to express the consummation of God uniting with the church.

It was not God that needed the woman–but the man. Why? Because of reproduction and the attribute of expression–man could not express God being alone. If God had stopped with Adam His manifesto would never have gotten off the ground. Man could not express all the synonyms and attributes of God being alone; there are two sides to God, and Adam and Eve were especially designed to express them individually.

When God fashioned the woman, His plan was that Adam would play His part and Eve the part of the church. Thus, when a man loves his wife it is an expression of God's love for His church. (John Chapter 17) explains it in the type of a father and son relationship.) And thus, when a woman loves her husband, it is an expression of the churches' love to God; it is a simple factor of divine nature expressed through rationality.

Since the first Adam crashed, the second Adam, Jesus Christ, is now our example of what God wanted us to be. God conveyed so much of Himself into the Body of Jesus that there was really nothing left of Himself outside that body: *"For* (saith the scripture) *in Him dwelleth all the fullness of the Godhead bodily."* And thus, since all the fullness of God dwelleth in Him–in that body, (Col 2:9) the only place you will find God is within the *Body of Jesus Christ*.

This is where man stumbles at the Deity of Jesus Christ: He was God manifested in the flesh. He was not another God, nor was He God the Son. He was none other than the very God of heaven, which was made into a man to fully and completely manifest and express Himself through the constitution of flesh: The unknown God: Inexpressible, Invisible, Indivisible Spirit manifested Himself in the flesh–that was easy.

"Who being the brightness of his glory, and the express image (The word *"image"* is a mystical expression relating to character and not that of human form) *of his person,* (His personification or personality) *and upholding all things by the word of his power,* (keeping everything under control in heaven above and on earth below) *when he had by himself purged our sins, sat down on the right hand of the majesty on high"* (as promised to David: A man, a God-Man, is now sitting upon the throne of David in heaven) (1 Kings 9:5). (A. W. Pink).[4]

The Apostle Paul explains it even more perfectly: *"For God, who commanded the light to shine out of darkness* (spiritual darkness) *hath shined in our hearts,* (by His Spirit) *to give the light* (the revelation) *of the knowledge to the glory of God in the face of Jesus Christ"* (2 Cor 4:6).

This brings us to this question: What do people see in your face? Do they hear His voice within your words? Do they see His Image within your character? Or does His image fade in and out to accommodate the situation?

This is why it is so important that man is transformed spiritually into the image of God, because without man, there is no other expression of God. Oh, yes, *"The heavens declare the glory of God; and the firmament sheweth his handiwork"* (Ps 19:1). But these are declarations and proclamations of His power and wisdom and temperament–but not of His Image.

As soon as the creation of man was revealed to the angels the devil began to investigate. Before this, the only beings existing were angels who were created to serve and worship God in the spirit world, and likewise man was created to worship

God from the earth world. But as soon as man was created a war for his devotion began in heaven. And as it has continued here on the earth, by the corrupt nature of man, it appears the devil is winning. However, the war for man's devotion is not over, as people from all walks of life and from every nation are receiving the gospel and are being transformed into the image of God.

O, the trust and the responsibility placed upon man that he should represent the very God of heaven here on earth! O, the accountability to answer the call to minister to such a corrupt domain! O, the example of God in the flesh set forth before our very eyes that we should stand in His stead as representatives of His *Divine Word*! O, the power and the glory entrusted into man's hands that he should symbolize His feet, His hands, His eyes, His heart, and His voice in a world so stained with sin! O, the aspiration experienced by knowing that *Jesus Christ is God*! O, the glory of becoming His life on earth and expressing His feelings to a lost world! O, the terrifying punishment worthy of those who trod under foot the divine commission wrought by His Blood!

You will not find God outside the Body of Jesus Christ, and neither will you find Him outside His *Holy Word*. Moreover, and as pathetic as it may appear, man is the only physical representative God has when it comes to expressing Himself to the world. Not a great choice but it is working. Would you lend Him your life today? He needs your hands, your feet, your eyes and your heart, to love an unlovable world. Why not lend Him your life today–the rewards are literally out of this world.

Chapter 27

The Mystery Of The Talking Snake

Among all the great paraphrases and illustrations found in the Bible, the one in (Gen 3:1-5) concerning the talking snake is the most fascinating; but something seems to be missing here that the scribes are not telling us. The creation of the earth is more an introduction of time, whereas the creation of man seems to hold a strange Preface: Are we to believe that this hissing crawling creature once walked and talked and stood upright? Are we to believe that this tetrapod (amphibious creature) and this tripartite (human being) were literally engaged in a conversation–conversing with an audible voice? Snakes do not talk–they hiss. But here we have a story of a human being conversing with a snake and the news of it made its way into the journals of religious history, (the Bible) which we were taught from a child to believe every word–*as it is written*. However, since I have been a Bible student for over fifty-years, I have learned that there are some things *written* that cannot be taken at face value.

When God created all these creatures, He created them to remain the same in nature as they were designed: dogs barked, birds chirped, cats meowed, cows mooed, chickens clucked, the roosters crowed, and the snake hissed. Oh, yes, there was one time when a mule spake with man's voice, (Numb 22:21-33 / 2 Peter 2:16). And what is the difference in a mule or a snake speaking with mans voice? Ask the mule or the snake.

Number One: The mule spake because God needed someone to warn a soothsaying prophet–has any of your animals been talking to you lately? Number Two: Surely you would not assert that it was the Spirit of God that anointed the snake to causally speak with man's voice? We know what the Bible says, but what we don't know is what is the Bible saying to us through these creature scenarios; thus, we fail to see the meaning behind the expressions. I have said this many times and so say I it again: The story in Genesis chapter-three is not a story about a talking snake. It is a story of how man was deceived by evil cunningness within his own mind, and the snake is here used as an example because of its crafty nature; the story is as much a parable as any other parable in the Bible.

Most Bible students are inclined to believe, that when God created the snake, it talked with man's voice and walked in some type of upright position? I think not. Reason One: God made no mention of change anywhere within His *written Word*–only in comparison to man (Matt 3:7, 23:33/2 Peter 2:16, 22). Reason Two: One would have to believe in the theory of Evolution to believe the snakes physical posture was changed. Reason Three: Snakes were created with a carnivorous appetite; they crave meat. Did the scribes make a mistake in what they wrote? No. God had something else in mind and it involved the church. The cursing of the snake: it crawling on its belly and eating dirt–all hold mysteries that Christians need to know about. Meanwhile, creation has not changed–if it did it left no evidence.

Our Lord called a man a Fox in (Luke 13:32). Are we to believe the man was a literal Fox? John, the Baptist` called some in his audience, Vipers (Matt 3:7/Luke 3:7). Are we to believe they were literal snakes? Gentiles were classified as dogs just as the Jews were as swines. Are we to believe they were literally thus? None of the above applies in the literal tense-sense; only literalists believe it as thus.

Our Lord spake many things in the tense of allegories and parables as character references in relating to the nature of man; He used many illustrations of which few existed in reality. They were transcending thoughts relating to the nature of the creature in comparison to the nature of man. Just as there are parables within the New Testament, there are parables also within the Old Testament.

Do not be deceived by the images projected within the writings you find in the Bible, they are mere shadows of the nature of creatures in relation to the nature of man. Because the Bible speaks of God having hands, feet, and eyes, etc., does not mean that He has these commodities. Because it is written in the Bible that: *"He shall cover thee with his feathers, and under his wings shalt thou trust"* (Ps 91:4). Does this mean that God is some type of feathered fowl? I think not.

So, where then did we get the ideal that God has the same essentials as man, and that man has the same nature as animals? Simple: It came from our imagination: Man's imagination has been restructured through the years through the theory of Telegenics instead of the *written Word of God*. Thus, man has conceived in his mind that God has the same essentials as man and animals–even the same intellect. This explains why we have a snake conversing with a human being; it is man's way of reasoning. But God is not subject to man's way of reasoning. The ideal of this crawling creature speaking with man's voice is an *anthropomorphic expression* written within the range of human reasoning.

Let the student notice that this creature is called the serpent instead of a snake. But that's not a problem, because, whether snake, serpent, or Satan, the titles are all synonymous in meaning and purpose. Just as there are many fairytales today, which paint pictures within our mind, there are also many strange expressions within the *Holy Scriptures* that do the same. So, with this thought in mind, let's wade out a little deeper.

After God had finished the creation of man and breathed into him the breath of life, then came the big challenge. God fooled around and fashioned a woman and that was when the story turned into suspense. Then one day God was relaxing on the clouds when He noticed that something had gotten Eve's attention; it was the tree with the forbidden fruit. She seemed to be in a doable state of mind as if someone was talking to her inner person.

(This happens a lot to Christians today who listen to voices that are not founded upon the *written* Word of God, and thus, they reach for forbidden fruit that has been labeled as poison.)

It must have been Satan speaking to her mind through the power of telepathy: Speaking without using words–speaking to the inner person through thought patterns, which produce word pictures–he's good at that.

This also is how God speaks to His people today–to their thoughts. You've heard the expression: "What they said really blew me away." Well, that's how it is between us humans and God; some of the things written within His book can really blow your mind. Nevertheless, or whichever, Satan got her attention and got his message across and she took the bait.

But the mystery of the talking serpent–how did that thought come to be? It came into existence when the scribes began their writings of the chronicles of creation. Remember, it was not until the days of Moses, some twenty-five hundred years later, that God anointed him and certain scribes to compile man's chronicles, including the creation. But by this time a lot of Egyptian Mythology had gotten into the bloodstream of the Israelites–including the holy scribes, and was passionately zealous among all in the land of Egypt, and the serpent was one of their gods.

There were all kinds of gods with all kind of shapes in Egypt, and curiosity is in the nature of man; Egypt's ideals of idol worship were the only mental pictures the scribes had to relate too. The scribes did not write in error while under the influence of the *Holy Spirit*; though mystifying, encrypted, strange, elusive, and at times incomprehensible, their writings were still written from a human point of view of things that existed in their day and time—yet their writings were accepted as infallible.

I know how this feels inside the mind and heart as a writer: Oceans of imaginary inspirations flood the mind and heart so forcibly that keeping up with the overflow of thoughts can feel impossible. Then we edit and remove all the scrip/scrap of what would appear fictitious, and then exhaust all the synonyms available. But these expressions were not written open-mindedly: The hand of the Spirit of God was behind the anointing, composing picture words within the range of the scribe's apprehension. There were many things I wanted to write about within my series of books; however, though I felt the Spirit of the Lord upon me, the scope of my apprehension forbade me.

This is when the power of *anthropomorphic expressions* was put into action to consolidate volumes into sentences. As I said above, creation has not evolved or changed since the day of creation: Dogs still bark, cows still moo, birds still chirp, and people still talk and walk and think. But let's break this down and put it into a dictionary thought: "*Anthropomorphism* is any attribution of human characteristics assumed to belong only to humans or abstract concepts, such as animals with abilities to reason and converse. The term was coined in the mid 1700s…as a literary device; *Anthropomorphism* is strongly associated with art and storytelling…such as with animals as characters that can stand, walk and talk, and is commonly recognized with human behavior."[2]

This is how we got our story-telling ideals of cartoons with talking creatures; it is man speaking through these lifeless animations. In religion and Mythology, *Anthropomorphism* refers to the perception of a divine being in human form, or the recognition of human qualities within these beings.

Man is an *Anthropus,* which means, man is human. *Morphic* or *Morphism* means man has a form. Thus we have the word "*Anthropomorphic*" man with a form, or, an animal with human attributes."[2] God is not *anthropomorphic.* However, He uses *anthropomorphic expressions* when communicating with man. It is a transcending illustration factor from *Deity* to humanity–from *Spirit* to flesh–from His world to ours–from up there to down here; God has tossed man a rope through these expressions if only man could grasp it.

Allow me to express this in modern day terminologies: After God saw how man through the woman was deceived; He decided to have it explained. God gave man over two thousand years to study his world before He entrusted him to write about it. Since therefore the serpent was the most cunning of all His creatures, (as his name means "guise of evil") it was chosen as an example of the nature of evil because of its cunning devises. The serpent speaking with man's voice is an expression only because serpents do not talk. If they spoke in the beginning of time then why aren't they speaking yet today? Creation has not changed. If you believe the snake talked with mans voice and walked upright, then you are a realist who believes in evolution and your mind is without depth. It was a mindboggling attack from within the heart of the beholder that confused Eve's sense of obedience until she could not resist the temptation. Her heart and mind was under a cyber attach (if you please) that was spawned by the desires of the flesh, and has since been an optical elusion to all mankind; the lust of the eye took control just as it does today while entertaining evil thoughts. Thoughts have put a body on God, made spirits visible, changed the course of nature, exalted the animal world to divinity, and reduced man to the level of a snake–all through the power of imaginary Telegenics (replacing man's thoughts with pictures).

The eating of dirt and crawling on its belly are expressions of how low a human being will stoop and what he will choose as food for his soul. I can understand that: There have been many times in my life that I have had to eat some of the dirt I stirred up because of my lack of knowledge. Not in the literal tense-sense, but in the form of humility–Perhaps you too have been there–done that.

CONCLUDING THOUGHTS

The curvatures of thoughts within this book have been mind-boggling beyond degree; its intrusive intense research and deep meditations was frustrating to the integrity of my intellect. Nevertheless, through the power of prayer and the inspiration of the *Holy Ghost* suggestively resting upon me, I at last have completed my task of partially explaining how to find the answers hidden behind *anthropomorphic expressions*.

I was asked concerning the nature of this book: "Who, and what type of people will purchase and read this eccentric scrip?" My reply: "People who want to know more about God. People who want to fly higher and dive deeper into the unknown intellect of the spirit world." I spent years reading and studying the writings of Charles H. Spurgeon, St. John Chrysostom, A. W. Pink, R. C. Trench, Marcus Rainsford, J.I. Packer, John Owen, Bishop. John H. Vincent, Adolph Saphir, and many other syndicated writers. What was I looking for–the answers to so many unsolved mysteries. Man will never experience God any higher or deeper than his knowledge of God. The opportunity to learn about God and eternity is all around us; yet man continually rejects the counsel of God.

This book has been a majestic challenge as well as a noble accomplishment and one that I shall never forget or regret.

Thank you for reading my book, and may God's riches blessings be upon you.

Author, *Benjamin Lee Vince*

INDEX

(1) Encarta® World English Dictionary © 1999 Micro soft Corporation. All rights reserved. Developed for Microsoft by Bloomsbury Publishing PLC.

(2) Wikipedia Free Encyclopedia.

(3) Suggested citation for this article: Ignaz Philipp Semmelweis (1818-65) July 21, 2014. Centers for Disease Control and Prevention 1600 Clifton Rd, NE, Mailstop D61 Atlanta, GA 30333…<u>all materials published in Emerging Infectious Diseases are in the Public Domain and can be used without permission. Proper citation, however, is required</u>. Reference Link: (wwwnc.cdc.gov/eid/article/7/2/pdfs/ac-0702.pdf).

(4) A. W. Pink: Gleanings from Genesis, V1. Copyright: A. C. Gaebelein 1922, P11, P14, P17-18, Publication Office "Our Hope" 456 Fourth AVE, New York, N.Y. Public Domain. QUOTE: "There is a wide difference between *creating* and *making*: To create is to call into existence something out of nothing; to *make* is to form or fashion something out of materials already existing."

QUOTE: "Behind him was no sinful heredity, within him was no deceitful and wicked heart, upon him were no marks of corruption, and around him were no signs of death." P14.

QUOTE: "The words *Theophany* or *Theophanic* are expressions of manifestations: "Man is a Tripartite being: he is made up of spirit, soul, and body, (1 Thess 5:23). The late Dr. Pierson distinguished them as thus: "The spirit as God-consciousness, the soul as the seat of self-consciousness, and the body as sense-consciousness." P17-18.

A.W. Pink: Exposition in 1. John. P68, No ISBN, No Copyright date, No address, No contact, Associated Publishers and Authors, Inc. (Baker Publishing Co) Grand Rapids, MI.49315. Rule of permission: 250 words per book (Used by permission).

A.W. Pink: Exposition of Hebrews, by P513, Copyright 1st 1954, 18th 1994. Publisher: Baker Book House, Grand Rapids, MI. Copyright # 54-11076 Copyright date: 1954. ISBN 0-8010-6857-6

(5) "Exploring the nature of Omnipresence" by Jason Dulle. Jasondulle@yahoo.com (Used by permission).

(6). New Self-Interpreting Bible Library Vol II Judges–Song of Solomon, by Bishop John H. Vincent, (1832-1920) Copyright 1909. (Public Domain) Vol IV, Column 1. P256.

(7) Charles H. Spurgeon: Lectures To My Students, P9, P50, P179 publisher: Old Time Gospel Hour, Lynchburg, Virginia. ISBN: 0-8407-4165-0 1875, 1877, 1894, (Used by permission.)

(8) Bishop M.M. Hudson, unpublished document–deceased.

(9) W.E. Vine Expository Dictionary of New Testament Words (Pages: 148, 279, 280, 281). Published by Fleming H Company, Old Tappan, New Jersey. 1st published 1940, 17th 1966–No copyright date) Now Baker Publishing Co. Rules of permission: 250 words per book (Used by permission).

QUOTES: "Repentance helps us to express its meaning in perhaps a more intellectual or accurate way.

As a Verb: It helps us to perceive the implying change of the mind.

As an Adjective: It speaks of God in regard to his gifts and calling, (Rom 11:29).

As a Noun: Repentance is an after thought of regret...To amend or resolve one's life as a result of contrition for one's sins."

(10) Saint John Chrysostom: NPNF1-12. Homilies on the Epistles of Paul to the Corinthians by St. John Chrysostom Title: URL: Author(s): Publisher: Print Basis: Rights: Date Created: Status: CCEL Subjects: NPNF1-12. Saint Chrysostom: Homilies on the Epistles of Paul to the Corinthians http://www.ccel.org/ccel/schaff/npnf112.html Schaff, Philip (Editor) Grand Rapids, MI: Christian Classics Ethereal Library Edinburgh: T&T Clark, 1889 Public Domain 2002-05-21

This document has been carefully proofed All; Early Church; Sermons–"His Body."

St. John Chrysostom: Volume XXV, 1&2 Corinthians, Water Baptism, Homily XXIV. 1 Cor 10:13, copyright 1909, (PDF Copy–Public Domain).

St. John Chrysostom: Homily–Volumes X, XI, XII. XIII, XIV, (Early church father) Baker Publishing Group–copyright 1909, (Public Domain).

(11) "The Bible, re-write it or re-read it", Chap 10, *Those Dumb Fisherman*, by Benjamin Lee Vince. Pb: AuthorHouse. Cr: 2010/2014, ISBN: 978-1-44906-827-1 (Author–Owner).

(12) Miracles & Parables of the Old Testament by R C Trench, P395-396, Published by Baker House, copyright 1890, 1959, 1974, card # 59-8345. Rules of permission: 250 words per book, (Used by permission).

(13) Adolph Saphir 1831-1891: "Christ & the Scripture" P64 No Copyright date, Published by Montrose Christian Literature Society, Montrose, PA, Date unknown–Public Domain.

(14) Cover by *THE IMAGE HOUSE Inc.* Alan E. Ray, owner (No longer in business, author-owner.

OTHER BOOKS BY BENJAMIN LEE VINCE

1. *ANGELVISION -VS- TELEVISION*
(Telegenics and the Weapon of Mass-Distraction)
Published 2006/2012
ISBN: 978-1-4685-1043-0 (sc)
ISBN 978-1-4685-1044-7 (e)

2. *THE BIBLE, RE-WRITE IT OR RE-READ IT*
(Generic Bibles Begat Generic Christians)
Published 2010/2014
ISBN: 978-1-4343-8304-4 (sc)
ISBN: 978-1-46783-480-3 (e)

3. *GOLIATH AWAITS*
(When God Doesn't Make Sense)
Published 2010
ISBN: 978-1-4343-8304-4
ISBN 978-1-44906-828-8 (e)

4. *DAVID THE WARRIOR / DAVID THE POLITICIAN*
(When The Ministry Turns To Politics For Their Answer)
Published 2014
ISBN: 978-1-49691-367-8 (sc)
ISBN: 978-1-49691-368-5 (e)

~ BOOKS IN PROCESS ~

6. *SEVERING THE TIES*
(When Love Is Etched In Stone)

VISIT: www.goliathbookseries.com/

Printed by BoD™in Norderstedt, Germany